WHAT YOUR COLLEAGUES ARE SAYING . . .

"Schools are a community, and all communities experience challenges and success. One of the challenges we commonly face is supporting our educators in understanding how to meet our students' social-emotional and behavioral needs in a way that provides proactive and sustainable solutions. *The Restorative Practices Playbook* is an outstanding resource any educator can use to start their journey toward positive change. This book is full of practical tools and examples that can support an individual teacher or create systemwide change. I highly recommend this book to all educators."

—**Heath Peine,** Executive Director of Student Support Services, Wichita Public Schools

"I haven't been as excited about the implications of any book I have read as I have with *The Restorative Practices Playbook.* As we continue to evolve in our discipline methods as a district, this playbook offers a systematic guide that can help us to reflect and adjust our practices. We need to offer better solutions to support positive behavior in our schools, and this book provides action steps to make those changes happen."

—**Kris Felicello,** Superintendent of Schools, North Rockland Central School District

THE
RESTORATIVE PRACTICES PLAYBOOK

THE
RESTORATIVE PRACTICES PLAYBOOK

TOOLS FOR **TRANSFORMING DISCIPLINE** IN SCHOOLS

DOMINIQUE SMITH
DOUGLAS FISHER
NANCY FREY

Foreword by
ZACHARY SCOTT ROBBINS

CORWIN

Fisher & Frey

FOR INFORMATION:

Corwin

A SAGE Company

2455 Teller Road

Thousand Oaks, California 91320

(800) 233-9936

www.corwin.com

SAGE Publications Ltd.

1 Oliver's Yard

55 City Road

London EC1Y 1SP

United Kingdom

SAGE Publications India Pvt. Ltd.

B 1/I 1 Mohan Cooperative Industrial Area

Mathura Road, New Delhi 110 044

India

SAGE Publications Asia-Pacific Pte. Ltd.

18 Cross Street #10-10/11/12

China Square Central

Singapore 048423

President: Mike Soules

Vice President and
  Editorial Director: Monica Eckman

Director and Publisher,
  Corwin Classroom: Lisa Luedeke

Senior Content Development
  Manager: Julie Nemer

Associate Content Development
  Editor: Sarah Ross

Editorial Assistant: Nancy Chung

Production Editor: Melanie Birdsall

Typesetter: C&M Digitals (P) Ltd.

Proofreader: Lawrence W. Baker

Cover Designer: Gail Buschman

Marketing Manager: Deena Meyer

Printed in the United States of America

ISBN 978-1-0718-8458-4

Library of Congress Control Number: 2022931835

This book is printed on acid-free paper.

22 23 24 25 26 10 9 8 7 6

CONTENTS

③ ESTABLISHING EXPECTATIONS AND TEACHING FOR ENGAGEMENT — 47

④ RESTORATIVE CONVERSATIONS USING AFFECTIVE STATEMENTS — 67

Visit the companion website at
resources.corwin.com/restorativepracticesplaybook
for downloadable resources, tools, and guides.

FOREWORD

Restorative justice work is social justice work. In *The Restorative Practices Playbook*, Dominique Smith, Douglas Fisher, and Nancy Frey highlight the power of genuine positive relationships among students and adults in schools. The authors provide readers with practical tools to encourage a sense of belonging and to foster connectedness among school community members. They provide readers with a toolkit to help educators feel safe being vulnerable to students and with each other and to allow students to be vulnerable and accept responsibility. These practices reduce conflict and enable schools to handle conflict in productive ways that emphasize growth, development, and learning rather than isolation and punishment.

In *The Restorative Practices Playbook,* the authors show readers how restorative practices positively impact schools and school-related outcomes. Students benefit from classrooms that function in predictable ways with predictable routines facilitated by a teacher they can trust to treat them with a predictable level of kindness and care. Even when events upend students' worlds outside of school, students must trust schools and the adults responsible for making schooling happen in ways that provide them with predictable routines and learning.

Dominique Smith, Douglas Fisher, and Nancy Frey show readers how restorative justice practices provide structures, processes, and functions schools can use to make things right when someone disrupts the school environment. These practices allow community members to repair harms and restore fractured relationships among each other. When done well, restorative practices help school community members protect core values and instructional time by diverting students from suspensions and expulsions and keeping them in classrooms. It is imperative that we keep all kids in school and ensure all students have equitable access to a free and appropriate public education.

I first met Doug Fisher and Nancy Frey the same way as many of you reading this foreword. I met them through their work. Before becoming an author, school principal, and professor, I was an English teacher. I knew Dr. Fisher and Dr. Frey through their research and writing on improving students' reading comprehension and writing. Later in my career, a high school I was leading got accepted into a competency-based education pilot program, which complemented a dual enrollment program I was determined to build with support from community partners. I dug deeper into Dr. Fisher and Dr. Frey's work at Health Sciences High and Middle College (HSHMC) to get curricular ideas and insight to revamp my school's curricular program. Connecting with Dr. Fisher and Dr. Frey through this foreword and other academic work is the universe working in mysterious ways.

Some time ago, I met Dr. Dominique through Twitter. (I'm not even kidding.) Dr. Dominique Smith is a school leader at HSHMC, and he sent a few members of his staff to hear me talk about my work in restorative justice. I connected with them, but I wasn't able to connect with Dominique at that time. Now, Dr. Dominique is "my dawg." For those who may not understand that colloquialism, Dr. Dominique and I have a wonderful appreciation for each other. Dr. Dominique and I connected about restorative justice online, via telephone, and it was clear that we were like-minded.

The work that this team has done on *The Restorative Practices Playbook* will help many children, educators, and schools. The ideas in the manuscript are wonderfully presented. The messaging about mindfulness, collaboration, and agency is needed. The playbook is written in an informative, easy-to-read style. Educators will find it a fantastic resource for reflection and action planning, particularly educators and school leaders new to restorative practices.

I do want to note that this book does not seek to take a deep dive into the intersections of race, implicit bias, and restorative practices. This book isn't written for that purpose. This is not the book that intends to explore restorative justice where it is equally (sometimes mortally) essential to be culturally competent as it is to be competent in one's subject matter pedagogy to be effective. This isn't that book. There are other books about restorative justice that immerse readers in discussions about the intersections of disproportionality, systemic discrimination, and restorative practices.

My colleagues have written a book that is exemplary at doing what it is designed to do. *The Restorative Practices Playbook* helps educators start or continue their restorative justice journeys, remain reflective about their practice, and make refinements to stay on track in their efforts. I am confident that *The Restorative Practices Playbook* will give schools tools to take important steps along their path to restorative practice.

My ministry in this restorative justice work is anchored in the belief that Jim Crow disciplinary practices in schools must end. Restorative justice provides waypoints to derail Jim Crow disciplinary outcomes. In this spirit, Dominique Smith, Douglas Fisher, and Nancy Frey provide readers with *The Restorative Practices Playbook*. This playbook is timely and much needed.

—**Zachary Scott Robbins**
School Principal, Clark County School District

ACKNOWLEDGMENTS

Corwin gratefully acknowledges the contributions of the following reviewers:

Kris Felicello
Superintendent of Schools
North Rockland Central School District
Garnerville, NY

Heath Peine
Executive Director of Student Support Services
Wichita Public Schools
Wichita, KS

Zachary Scott Robbins
School Principal
Clark County School District
Las Vegas, NV

INTRODUCTION

Clarke is a new student who is very excited and a bit nervous about the new school. Clarke attended a rural, or as they say, "country school," for several years. You find out Clarke's father is a well-known farmer who is taking a role at the corporate office in the city. Clarke has worked on the farm for years and has lots of stories about equipment, animals, and crops. Clarke is especially fond of milk cows and wrote about the taste of fresh milk during a quick write. On the second day of attending the new school, someone realizes Clarke has a knife on the back of their belt.

Given your current school or district rules, what are you required to do? What course of action is required of you? Clearly, a rule has been broken and Clarke created an unsafe environment. As we will explore throughout this book, a punitive approach focused on the following questions:

- What law or rule was broken?
- Who broke it?
- What punishment is deserved?

In this case, Clarke clearly violated an important rule related to school safety. The question then is, what is the punishment? In many places, Clarke would be suspended. In some places, Clarke might even be expelled. After all, there was a knife on campus that created an unsafe place to learn. Some will argue that Clarke will only learn if there are exclusionary consequences for this action.

Do you agree with this course of action, given what you know about Clarke? What do you wish would happen differently? We shared this example because we hope you are thinking that there is a much simpler solution and one that will likely ensure that Clarke learns not to bring a knife to school. But the situations you encounter are often much more complex than this. And they deserve the same type of investigation as to the *why* before considering a course of action.

Before we continue, let's consider another example. Nancy is at the airport and security pulls her bag from the line. They ask if there was anything sharp in her bag and Nancy replies, "No," not remembering that she had been helping a friend over the weekend and has a utility knife in her bag. Of course, security finds it and shows it to her. She apologizes profusely and then is suspended from flying ever again. Okay, the suspension part's not true. But they do ask if she wants to check the utility knife or throw it away. Once the problem is solved, they let her go on her way.

We are not advocating for weapons on campus (or airplanes) any more than we support students being disrespectful to teachers. But there are ways to ensure that students learn from the mistakes that they make. We are educators and our primary role is to teach. When students have unfinished learning, educators create opportunities for students to learn. Unfortunately, too often that role seems to stop when it comes to behavior:

If a student doesn't know how to read,

We teach that student how to read.

If a student doesn't know how to do math problems,

We teach that student to do math.

If a student doesn't know how to behave,

We punish that student.

Where is the teachable moment? Isn't that why we entered this most noble profession? To teach. That's what restorative practices are about. In this book, we focus on a set of practices that are designed to teach. That must include teaching prosocial behaviors based on strong relationships and a commitment to the well-being of others.

Before we continue, it's important to clear up a confusion. We have been asked far too many times, *What about consequences? Are there ever consequences for the actions that students take? What if they hurt someone? What if they destroy property?*

> THERE ARE WAYS TO ENSURE THAT STUDENTS LEARN FROM THE MISTAKES THAT THEY MAKE. WE ARE EDUCATORS AND OUR PRIMARY ROLE IS TO TEACH.

Restorative practices are about healing. They are about re-establishing the learning environment. Of course, there are consequences. That may even include time away from school for calming down and making plans. We just understand that some of the traditional consequences that schools use do not result in any new learning.

Doug's high school English teacher was frustrated with one of Doug's writing assignments. In front of the whole class, the teacher told Doug that he would spend the rest of his life "flipping burgers." Frustrated and hurt, Doug threw a pencil at the wall and walked out of class. He was then sent to the principal, who asked if Doug had done what was written on the referral, which he admitted. Doug was suspended for three days. No one at school asked Doug why he did it. What did Doug learn from this suspension? Well, one thing he learned was to never trust that teacher. Doug missed that class a lot after that day but made up the grade in the summer. The hurt and lack of belief that the teacher showed were never addressed. Perhaps the teacher intended something else and a quick conversation could have resolved the feelings. Perhaps the teacher had not considered the impact of a statement made in frustration and a conversation could have enlightened that teacher. What if Doug had heard that his actions scared the teacher and had a chance to learn about the impact of his actions? Why were so many opportunities missed? Opportunities to spend time figuring out what went wrong, why, and how to resolve it.

So where do we start? How might we create restorative classrooms and schools? It starts with *why*. But, although we could, we are not going to provide you with an extensive literature review about the impact of restorative practices. We don't find that as compelling as asking you: What is your *why*? When you find your *why*, you will know how restorative practices can help you accomplish your vision.

Simon Sinek's "Start With Why" is among the most-watched TED Talks. His message is clear: your *why* is what drives you and gives you purpose. So, what is your *why*? When is the last time you thought about it? Consider the following prompts. Take some time to reflect and add your own thoughts.

RESTORATIVE PRACTICES ARE ABOUT HEALING. THEY ARE ABOUT RE-ESTABLISHING THE LEARNING ENVIRONMENT.

Why did you become an educator?	
What makes you a great teacher or leader?	
What do you hope for your students?	
What goals do you have for yourself as an educator?	

We have asked countless numbers of people a simple but most meaningful question: *Why are you an educator?* Again and again, individuals light up and tell us their *why* with a story:

- For the kids

- To be the adult I never had

- To be just like my third-grade teacher who saved my life

- To fight for students with disabilities because my brother didn't have a chance

- To make a difference in the lives of others

- To showcase that learning is fun

- To share science in a way it has never been seen before

- To allow *all* voices to be heard

- To help create the next generation

- To see a student's eyes light up when they finally get it

- To change lives

- My family were all educators and I knew I could make a difference

- To give students a person they can count on

As we read these *whys* and reflect on our own, we see a trend. Educators come into this profession for the love, care, and ongoing growth of students. These are known as the moral rewards of teaching. And they are a powerful force for satisfaction in our roles and the generally positive feelings we have about our chosen work.

WHAT MIGHT BE DIFFERENT IF THE VALUED ADULTS IN A YOUNG PERSON'S LIFE REMAINED AND WORKED THROUGH THE TROUBLE?

Dominique's *why* has always been *to be that adult who doesn't leave.* In part, restorative practices allow him to realize his *why*. Far too often, adults leave when students get in trouble. What might be different if the valued adults in a young person's life remained and worked through the trouble? What if we came to understand that exclusionary practices prevent us from realizing our *why*? That there are more effective ways for building, maintaining, and repairing relationships. And that there are rewards that come from watching students learn how to navigate the complex words of social skills and relationships. As Dominique says,

I get to listen to students.

I get to hear their stories.

I get to ensure that students have another chance.

Importantly, restorative practices are not just a way to create long-term change in students. These practices are fortifying for you, the educator, who has the opportunity to address the intentional and unintentional harm that inevitably comes from supporting the development of other humans. In part, restorative practices allow you to have your say, to provide others an opportunity to make amends, and for you to leave school feeling good about your accomplishments.

Module 1

THE LOGIC OF RESTORATIVE PRACTICES

BELIEF STATEMENT

The foundation of restorative practices is a school culture that actively invests in relationships among students, staff, and the community.

A Dilemma

Tony Hall is a new staff member in a high school. The school is in an urban neighborhood, and there is a convenience store across the street where students often go to get food or drinks before school. Each day, a different staff member is assigned to stand outside before school to remind students to use the crosswalk instead of jaywalking.

Mr. Hall is standing outside on duty one morning when a student he didn't know jaywalks across the street to the convenience store. As the student comes back across the street, Mr. Hall calls to him to use the crosswalk. When the student ignores him, Mr. Hall approaches the student: "Hey! I asked you to use the crosswalk. You can't jaywalk across the street."

The student, who is already having a hard day due to an argument at home, failing a test during first period, and seeing some negative social media posts, replies, "Who are you?" Mr. Hall explains that he is new to the school and that the student needs to listen to what he says.

Annoyed and preoccupied with his own challenges from the day, the student replies, "You're nobody. Get out of my f***ing way!" and keeps walking toward class.

Shocked and offended by the student's disrespectful behavior and language, Mr. Hall immediately takes the student to the principal's office. Heated and upset, Mr. Hall explains the situation to the principal.

How should the principal handle the situation?

COMMON MISCONCEPTIONS

Chances are pretty good that you have found yourself in a similar situation as a student, a teacher, or an administrator. The thing about these heated moments is that each of us brings our own stew of experiences, mental models, and biases to the situation. And don't forget that these are fueled by the emotions of the moment as well as those that are lingering from earlier in the day. When situations arise that are unexpected, we tend to rely on mental shortcuts to help us make a quick decision. The problem is that these decision-making shortcuts can sometimes introduce errors (more about that idea later).

It's possible you have some biases about restorative practices. Perhaps you've heard about them in the news or have been part of a conversation about them with some other educators. We'd like to take on some of those misconceptions about restorative practices:

Misconception 1: Only schools with a small student population can have success with restorative practices. Larger schools have too many students to engage in that work.

Fact: Restorative practices can be used in schools of any size. Although a large school has a large student population, there are also more teachers/staff to help build more relationships with students.

Misconception 2: Restorative practices don't hold students accountable; students can say or do anything without consequences.

Fact: Restorative practices take student accountability to a higher level because students and teachers are engaged in collaborative conversations around choices, actions, and behaviors that can foster true personal growth and change.

Misconception 3: Students should come to school knowing how to behave appropriately.

Fact: Most children and youth mimic what they see modeled by adults at home or in their community of influence. If the adults in their lives don't model appropriate behavior or don't have a good understanding of positive social and emotional behavior, we can't expect students to come to school with those skills. We as educators need to teach behavior with the same commitment that we teach reading and mathematics.

Misconception 4: When students display negative or problematic behavior, they are doing so by conscience and purposeful choice.

Fact: Many students come to school having experienced trauma, adverse childhood experiences, conflicts of all sorts, and a host of other things that impact their automatic reactions and self-protection mechanisms. We need to address trauma and recognize how students present these experiences to educators.

Misconception 5: "I should only have to teach my academic content. Everything else that students need should come from their families or the counselors."

Fact: The reality is that if students' physical and emotional needs are not met first, it doesn't matter what else we try to teach them; they won't have the capacity to learn it. Restorative practices seek to support the whole child and the whole situation and create a safe and welcoming place for students to learn.

Misconception 6: Restorative practices are a set of strategies that are to be used for a finite amount of time.

Fact: Restorative practice work is ongoing in order to build relationships with students and create a safe environment for learning. Growth and change take time, and not all students respond right away.

Misconception 7: Engaging in restorative practices instead of expulsion or suspension condones violent or extreme behavior.

Fact: Removing a student for extreme behavior only sends the problem somewhere else—it doesn't solve anything. Restorative practices provide students a chance to change their behavior and provide the opportunity to get students the services and support they need to make lasting personal change.

Misconception 8: Restorative practices make it impossible to suspend or expel students for extreme behavior.

Fact: Restorative practices significantly enrich the toolkit educators have for maintaining a safe and orderly environment. They do not replace other tools, including disciplinary tools. However, the result of implementing restorative practices is that suspension and expulsion rates have the potential to drop significantly as other accountability systems are grown.

LEARNING INTENTIONS

- I am learning about the principles of restorative practices.
- I am learning about ways schools enact restorative practices.

SUCCESS CRITERIA

- I can explain a logic model for restorative practices.
- I can engage in reflective thinking about my own experiences.
- I can apply principles of restorative practices to scenarios.

WHERE DO RESTORATIVE PRACTICES COME FROM?

There are three major influences that inform restorative practices. The first influence is the most enduring and echoes indigenous cultures from all over the world. These ties are most apparent in Māori, Native American, and First Nations practices that place the community at the heart of problem resolution. Harm is understood at the collective level, not solely as a conflict between two individuals. Therefore, repairing harm requires the involvement of the community.

The second influence comes from the social sciences, particularly in mediation and resolution practices. The fields of social work, counseling, and psychology each draw on the importance of assisting people in identifying feelings, hurt, and harm, but also in moving them forward to find resolution and to make amends. The additive perspective is that participants can experience insights about themselves. They become better equipped to make future decisions because of their gained wisdom.

A third influence stems from the field of criminal justice. The term *restorative justice* is used to describe an alternative process that focuses on taking responsibility for actions as well as harm and for ensuring that victims are heard and are made an active part of the process. First used in the 1970s, restorative justice has proven to be a particularly effective dimension in the juvenile justice system. Police departments and school districts have also found it to be a bridge between two institutions in a young person's life. The focus of this book is on *restorative practices*, which encompass a broader array of proactive and preventative approaches. Having said that, restorative conferences and victim-offender dialogue draw on restorative justice lessons learned from a variety of organizations.

HARM IS UNDERSTOOD AT THE COLLECTIVE LEVEL, NOT SOLELY AS A CONFLICT BETWEEN TWO INDIVIDUALS. THEREFORE, REPAIRING HARM REQUIRES THE INVOLVEMENT OF THE COMMUNITY.

Each of these areas influences the important element of conflict resolution. However, restorative practices encompass far more than problematic behavior. In fact, initiatives that only focus on the conflict to the exclusion of building a restorative culture are doomed to fail. The trusting relationships needed to ensure that there is something worth restoring are simply not there. Restorative practices are a largely proactive approach that builds students' capacity to self-regulate, make decisions, and self-govern. Without these skills, often referred to as 21st-century skills or soft skills, students will not make the academic strides they need to achieve their aspirations. At the school level, restorative practices provide a pathway for bringing equitable discipline that reduces exclusion, improves the school climate, and "fosters a relationally driven school community" (Kervick et al., 2020, p. 155). The data are clear: Black and other minoritized students and students with disabilities experience disproportionate disciplinary actions, including suspension and expulsion (e.g., Gregory et al., 2010).

PRINCIPLES AND RESEARCH ABOUT RESTORATIVE PRACTICES

INITIATIVES THAT ONLY FOCUS ON THE CONFLICT TO THE EXCLUSION OF BUILDING A RESTORATIVE CULTURE ARE DOOMED TO FAIL.

The research about restorative practices holds that, when compared to more conventional disciplinary approaches, it can have a positive effect on students' ability to be accountable for their actions (Gregory et al., 2016). An interesting study of the perceptions of Black fifth- and eighth-grade students indicated that students believed that the use of circles, an important group practice, fostered their ability to take the perspectives of others and to resolve conflict through communication (Skrzypek et al., 2020).

Many schools have adopted restorative practices as a comprehensive way to address racial, ethnic, gender, and ability disparities in exclusionary discipline, especially suspensions and expulsions. Researchers have drawn a bright line between disciplinary disparities and academic disparities, calling it "two sides of the same coin" (Gregory et al., 2010, p. 59). More recently, restorative practices have been seen as an important conceptual bridge to other initiatives, such as multitiered systems of support (MTSS) and social-emotional learning efforts (González et al., 2019).

A LOGIC MODEL FOR RESTORATIVE PRACTICES

Restorative practices don't just happen—they require coordinated effort to fully benefit from the potential to change the way students experience schooling. One way to plan for this is to create a simple logic model. Logic models provide an overview of how your effort is supposed to work and describe what happens when the actions are accomplished (Julian, 1997). Others call this a theory of change or even a road map. Having a logic model allows you to

- Identify a common challenge
- Allocate resources
- Project the impact
- Monitor it for success

Some people find the use of a logic model helpful, as it outlines the resources and activities necessary to achieve the intended results (see Figure 1.1). For others, it is a way to be able to see how resources and activities are aligned with intended outcomes. It isn't sufficient to simply name a goal and state what the outcomes will be. After all, a goal without a plan is just a wish.

Figure 1.1 Restorative Practices Logic Model

Goal: Create a healthy school ecosystem that addresses the needs of each child and inspires joy for all.

OUR INTENDED WORK		OUR INTENDED RESULTS	
RESOURCES	**ACTIVITIES**	**OUTPUTS** *DIRECT BENEFITS*	**OUTCOMES** *INDIRECT BENEFITS*
*If we have access to these resources, **then** these activities can be completed.*			
	*If we successfully complete these activities, **then** these changes will occur as a direct result of the actions.*		
		*If the activities are carried out as designed, **then** these changes will result.*	
			*If participants benefit from our efforts, **then** other systems, organizations, or communities will change.*
• Leadership team comprising key stakeholders • School-based mental health professionals with appropriate caseloads • Assessment tools • Restorative practices training materials	• Compile assessment information • Analyze assessment results • Evaluate discipline policies • Invest in creating and maintaining a restorative culture • Create a plan to infuse restorative practices into core programs and initiatives • Educate staff on restorative practices, including affective statements and impromptu conversations • Define behaviors that are addressed via restorative *conversations* • Define behaviors that are addressed via restorative *conferences* • Provide ongoing training on best practices	• Increased social-emotional and academic attainment • Decreased discipline referrals • Reduced exclusionary discipline (suspension and expulsion) • Greater equity in disciplinary decisions • Increased sense of belonging by students • Circles are regularly used to address a range of topics, including academic, social, and behavioral issues • Decreased dropout rates • Increased school attendance of students and staff	• Improved school climate • Improved mental and physical health outcomes • Fewer health-risk behaviors • Fewer students involved in the juvenile criminal justice system • Improved job satisfaction for staff • Decreased disability labeling and diagnoses

WEAVING THE LOGIC OF RESTORATIVE PRACTICES INTO THE SCHOOL DAY

Restorative practices are built around an 80/20 model—they are 80% proactive and 20% reactive. Historically, school policies are punitive in nature, with the belief that the right reaction will change behavior. But anyone who has spent time in K–12 schools knows that punitive actions do not always produce the desired results in students. Traditional punitive consequences such as a referral, removal from class, detention, suspension, or even expulsion do not solve the problem because those actions don't address whatever the underlying issue is. Restorative practices seek to address the real issues, and although they may not be successful or restore closure 100 percent of the time, it's better than not trying at all.

MANY SCHOOLS HAVE ADOPTED RESTORATIVE PRACTICES AS A COMPREHENSIVE WAY TO ADDRESS RACIAL, ETHNIC, GENDER, AND ABILITY DISPARITIES IN EXCLUSIONARY DISCIPLINE, ESPECIALLY SUSPENSIONS.

Restorative practices can occur throughout the school day in both academic and nonacademic settings. Everyone in a school building—administrators, counselors, teachers, and staff—can utilize restorative practices to build relationships with students and create a safe and accepting school climate. When a restorative school climate is established, students trust the teachers and feel safe going to an adult for help if something is happening on campus that needs attention. There might be natural consequences for the situation, but students know that the adults aren't out to "get" them. They understand that the goal is to create a safe environment with quality learning experiences for everyone on campus.

WHAT'S YOUR HISTORY?

When it comes to discipline, we are each a product of our experiences and our professional learning. Let's take on that last one—professional education. Many of us had a college course in our preliminary teaching program called Classroom Management. Perhaps you learned about techniques such as writing names on the board, using clip charts, referrals, or a timeout corner. When you were hired, you read the district handbook for employees, which covered the disciplinary process. Most of all, you absorbed the informal (sometimes unspoken) practices you witnessed such as when to write a referral, which administrators might be more sympathetic to your position, and, based on the teachers' lounge chatter, who were the kids most likely to give you a run for your money.

But your experiences are not limited to those that have occurred as an adult working in a school. We'd like to invite you to reflect on your experiences in writing and share them with a small group of colleagues (see Figure 1.2). There is no need to disclose all the information, and we do not in any way want to cause you further distress. We do not want you to explore a deeply traumatizing event that caused you great harm but rather a time when you were wronged. If this activity is one you prefer not to engage with, please feel free to move on. We use this activity to explore the meaning of justice.

Figure 1.2 When You Were a Victim

Directions: Write about a time when you were wronged, intentionally or unintentionally. You do not need to disclose the circumstances. Only consider how you experienced what followed.

How did you feel?	
What questions did you want to ask the offender?	
What else did you want to say to them?	
Who or what could make things right for you?	
What would justice have looked like for you?	

Each of us has experienced intentional or unintentional harm. If the harm involved the legal system, the offender may have been punished. But punishment of the offender isn't the same as having some resolution. Victims often have unanswered questions: *Why me? What did I do? What were you thinking?* If that experience didn't have a resolution, it is likely to linger with you in a different way. We have done this activity many times with educators, and we are always struck by how often the incident dates back years. It is not uncommon for people to have unsettled feelings that are magnified because they weren't afforded the kind of closure they need. When there is no opportunity to make amends and commitments, the experience stays with us.

Each of us has also found ourselves in the role of the offender, whether intentionally or unintentionally. This is an uncomfortable truth that we must confront. In this next exercise (Figure 1.3), we invite you to consider a time when you have been the offender in someone else's story. This is only for your own reflective purposes. There is no need to engage in dialogue about it. The point of this is to explore what you mean by justice and to consider the ways in which restorative practices can help address the unmet needs that we all have when it comes to harm. And that includes our students.

Figure 1.3	When You Were an Offender

Directions: For your reflection, write about a time when you were the offender, intentionally or unintentionally. This is a time when you did something wrong—something you're not proud of—and you got caught.

How did you feel?	
What would you have liked to say to the victim?	
Who or what would have made things right?	
What would justice have looked like for you and for the victim?	

This experience may have caused other emotions for you. The most common response we hear is that people would have liked to apologize to the person they caused harm to. Resolution works both ways. The opportunity to own our own behavior when we are not our best selves, to apologize and to receive a degree of forgiveness, as well as to make a commitment not to engage in that behavior again, gives us some important tools for how we move forward.

A RESTORATIVE CULTURE

The core of restorative practices centers on a restorative culture. It begins with the wisdom and the humility to acknowledge that we have found ourselves as victim and offender at various times throughout our life. Further, it is predicated on the knowledge that young people are learning about the social world—not just the physical and biological worlds we teach our students about in our classes. Educators model for students how to walk with grace through the world: we create classroom structures that foster a sense of belonging and we use language that builds students' sense of agency so that they can pursue their goals and aspirations. We teach them the prosocial skills needed to be accepted by peers. In these cases, efforts to help them label emotions and solve problems in order to improve relationships with peers may be necessary. We create classrooms and schools that allow students to govern what happens through shared decision making and exercising choice responsibility. And when faced with more significant conflict, we guide them to advocate for themselves and others, take responsibility, and make amends. These efforts are nested within one another at the individual, classroom, and school levels. Using Figure 1.4, take a few minutes to reflect on these efforts undertaken by you and your colleagues. What environments do you see occurring at your school?

THE GOAL IS TO CREATE A SAFE ENVIRONMENT WITH QUALITY LEARNING EXPERIENCES FOR EVERYONE ON CAMPUS.

Figure 1.4 A Restorative Culture Inventory

Directions: What evidence do you have that these efforts are happening at your school? What do you notice about strengths? Are there gaps that exist?

	WHAT DO I DO AS AN INDIVIDUAL TO FOSTER THIS CONDITION?	WHAT HAPPENS AT THE CLASSROOM LEVEL TO REINFORCE THIS CONDITION?	WHAT SCHOOLWIDE EFFORTS SUPPORT THIS CONDITION?
Belonging			

(Continued)

(Continued)

	WHAT DO I DO AS AN INDIVIDUAL TO FOSTER THIS CONDITION?	WHAT HAPPENS AT THE CLASSROOM LEVEL TO REINFORCE THIS CONDITION?	WHAT SCHOOLWIDE EFFORTS SUPPORT THIS CONDITION?
Language of agency and goal setting			
Prosocial skills			
Governance and decision making			
Addressing conflict			

HOW RESTORATIVE AM I?

While restorative practices are commonly viewed as a schoolwide initiative, their successful implementation is the product of individual efforts. We want to say first that one's ability to embody a restorative mindset is not static. We are humans before we are educators. Our health, the amount of sleep we got the night before, the personal and family worries and concerns we carry on our shoulder . . . these all influence our ability to enact a restorative mindset on any given day. Having said that, we are also subject to the mental shortcuts we take when interacting with students. These can be worsened when both we and the student are not our best selves.

Those mental shortcuts are called heuristics—think of these as "rules of thumb." Our brains are hard-wired to seek out patterns and associations to help us make sense of our surroundings. We exercise this cognitive process at an early age. We use these patterns to establish shortcuts that become increasingly complex as we age. These cognitive shortcuts help us make rapid decisions, which can be a very good thing. A long time ago, our ancestors used bias to make split-second decisions as to who is friend and who is foe. As our society, living conditions, and brains matured, contemporary humans co-opted the use of bias(es) as cognitive shortcuts to simplify our workloads. We create "mental scales" to weigh, disproportionately, in favor of or against certain ideas, opinions, purchases, interactions, friends, etc. (the list could go on forever). The point is that not all these cognitive shortcuts are bad. Oftentimes, we use them to help navigate the ever-busy day we experience as teachers (and humans). Unfortunately, our shortcuts can lead to a deficit mindset and overgeneralizations that can have a negative impact on the students and communities we serve. To complicate this topic even more, consider that these mental processes can happen unconsciously within the complex and hidden mechanics of our brains.

We can bring these cognitive shortcuts to our interactions with students. We invite you to reflect on your patterns when it comes to interacting with a student with whom you have a conflict. We're not talking about a serious conflict that has reached the point where others are involved. Instead, consider the pattern of interactions in those garden-variety annoying situations. This type of conflict has occurred when the usual redirection hasn't worked. Instead, the problem has persisted—a student is on her cell phone too much, a child continues to talk to his peers at his table even though you've instructed him to be quiet, or a student is just not doing the task you asked of them. Now complete the self-assessment below to reflect on your interactions.

WHEN THERE IS NO OPPORTUNITY TO MAKE AMENDS AND COMMITMENTS, THE EXPERIENCE STAYS WITH US.

SELF-ASSESSMENT: HOW RESTORATIVE AM I?

Directions: Reflect on how, in your role, you deal with students (or staff) when an incident or issue has arisen. Answer the questions below by marking a check in the column choices of *No, Not Often, Usually,* or *Always.*

	NO	NOT OFTEN	USUALLY	ALWAYS
1. Do I remain calm during the conversation?				
2. Do I really listen, without interrupting?				

(Continued)

	NO	NOT OFTEN	USUALLY	ALWAYS
3. Does the student understand why they are having this conversation?				
4. Would the student say I am a good listener?				
5. Do we explore how the school values apply to the issue?				
6. Does the student understand the harm they've caused, who has been affected, and how?				
7. Do I talk about how the incident affects me?				
8. Do I take responsibility for any part I might have played when things went wrong, acknowledge it, and apologize?				
9. Do I consider the extent to which I have a relationship with this student and how that affects my expectations for our interaction?				
10. If the student apologizes to me, do I accept the apology respectfully?				
11. Do I collaborate with the student to formulate a plan?				
12. Have I, at any stage, asked someone I trust to observe my practice and give me honest feedback?				
13. Do I try to handle most issues or incidents myself?				
14. Do I seek support when issues get tricky for me?				
15. Do I follow the school's systems when looking for more support?				
16. Is the relationship with the student repaired?				

Source: Positive Behaviour for Learning (2014a, p. 15). Adapted from "How restorative am I?" © Margaret Thorsborne and Associates, 2009.

Now that you have reflected on your experiences, what does this mean? Take a few minutes to analyze your responses and consider the questions that follow.

What patterns have you noticed?	
What strengths do you have?	
What areas of growth do you foresee?	

A DILEMMA: TAKE TWO

Let's revisit Mr. Hall's interaction with the jaywalking student before school to see how the principal helped build a restorative school climate. Recall that both Mr. Hall and the student are in the principal's office.

First, the principal asks the student to step outside her office and take a seat; she would come to talk to him in a few minutes. Then she asks Mr. Smith to do the same in her office. She asks Mr. Hall how he was feeling in that moment and how he felt now. The principal explains that many of the students have difficult situations outside of the classroom and that at this school, they practice restorative conversations to help build and repair relationships. She notes that this did not excuse the student's choice of language or disrespect and promises to address that as part of the conversation.

She then allows the student to come back into her office and facilitates a conversation between him and Mr. Hall. During

ONE'S ABILITY TO EMBODY A RESTORATIVE MINDSET IS NOT STATIC. WE ARE HUMANS BEFORE WE ARE EDUCATORS.

the conversation, the student shares that he hadn't eaten the previous night or that morning and was just trying to get something to eat before school. He also explains that he had had a difficult interaction with someone before even getting to school, and Mr. Hall just happened to be the next person "in line." Mr. Hall also has the opportunity to explain his perspective and how he felt disrespected in the way that the student approached the interaction, and together the three of them work to repair the situation.

Throughout that year, as Mr. Hall encounters that student around campus, their interactions are different because they came from a place of mutual understanding.

PROCEDURES

As you read this book, you will find support for creating restorative practices around the following key concepts, as illustrated in Figure 1.5:

WE STRIVE TO CREATE AN ACADEMIC ENVIRONMENT THAT ALLOWS YOUNG PEOPLE TO PURSUE GOALS AND ASPIRATIONS.

- A **restorative culture** informs the language we use to build agency and identity. We strive to create an academic environment that allows young people to pursue goals and aspirations. To create a restorative culture, we attend to the ways we build teacher credibility, set high expectations, and foster positive relationships with each member of the school community.

- **Restorative conversations** equip adults and students with the capacity to resolve problems, make decisions, and arrive at solutions in ways that are satisfactory and growth-producing for all. This requires cognitive reframing to deepen understanding of perspectives, using affective statements and impromptu conversations.

- **Restorative circles** are tools for prompting academic learning through dialogue, building community, making class decisions, and reaching resolution through healing. Each type of circle has its own set of protocols that are aligned to the purpose.

- **Restorative conferences** include formal meetings meant to foster guided dialogue between the victim(s) and offender(s). These conferences include plans for re-entry into the school community and involve other adults and students affected by the conflict.

Restorative practices encompass large and small interactions between educators, students, and families. Read the following scenario and consider what advice you have for the teacher and the school.

Figure 1.5 Restorative Practices

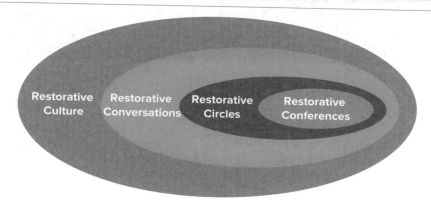

Restorative Culture

- Foundations of Respect
- High Expectations

Restorative Conversations

- Affective Statements
- Impromptu Conversations

Restorative Circles

- Circles

Restorative Conferences

- Victim-Offender Dialogue

CASE IN POINT

Jacob is a student in Mr. Abram's sixth-grade class. Jacob tends to be late to school, which often leads to him not having enough time to complete his morning bell ringer practice activities. This week has been a hard week. Jacob showed up 10 minutes late on Monday, 15 minutes late on Tuesday, and 8 minutes late on Wednesday. The school policy is that after a third tardy, the student loses lunch recess privileges for a day. Jacob pleads and says it's his mom making him late.

What do you think Mr. Abram should do?

MODULE 1

RECOMMENDATIONS AND IMPLICATIONS

We have created a table of general recommendations for consideration. Add your own site-specific implications and questions that this module has provoked for you.

	BROAD RECOMMENDATIONS	SITE-SPECIFIC IMPLICATIONS AND QUESTIONS
Schoolwide	Take an inventory of processes already in place to build on and to identify where gaps remain.	
Leaders	Hold conversations with teachers, parents, and students to gain insight into their knowledge and impressions about restorative practices.	
Teachers	Monitor your restorative conversations with students to notice your own current practices.	
Students	Examine your existing school climate survey data with restorative practices in mind. How might students' responses inform the school?	
Family and Community	Talk with family representatives about their knowledge and impressions of restorative practices to gain initial feedback.	

REFLECTION

Let's review the success criteria from the opening of this module. Ask yourself: Can you do these things now? Write your reflections below.

Can I explain a logic model for restorative practices?	
Can I engage in reflective thinking about my own experiences?	
Can I apply principles of restorative practices to scenarios?	

online resources

Access resources, tools, and guides
for this module at the companion website:
resources.corwin.com/restorativepracticesplaybook

MODULE 2

FOUNDATIONS OF RESPECT

BELIEF STATEMENT

Establishing a strong foundation of respect in the classroom and school fosters students' well-being and their eagerness to engage in restorative practices.

A Dilemma

It's the first day of school. Janet Clark has planned several "get-to-know-you" activities to begin the day and help her students learn about each other. She is really excited to build her students' sense of self and allow them to share what makes them special as they grow together as a community of learners.

As the students enter her class, they begin working on a "Who Am I?" poster. There are markers, crayons, and colored pencils available for the students to choose from, and everyone seems engaged as they work on the project.

When everyone has arrived, Ms. Clark begins to take attendance. Most of the students' names in her class she can pronounce easily. She politely asks a few students to say their names, and upon repeating what the students say, she is able to pronounce their names correctly.

Toward the end of the class roster, she comes upon one name that she isn't sure how to pronounce. The name is "Arundhathi Patel." To avoid butchering the name, she says, "Miss Patel, can you please tell me how to pronounce your name?" The student seems shy and soft-spoken but agrees to say her name aloud. Ms. Clark, earnestly trying to say the name correctly, is unsuccessful in a couple attempts to pronounce Arundhathi's name.

Embarrassed that she cannot get the pronunciation correct and not wanting to further put the student on the spot, Ms. Clark remarks, "I don't want to keep saying your name incorrectly. How about we come up with a nickname for you this year instead?"

Slouching into her seat with her head down, Arundhathi politely agrees to be called "Dottie" for the rest of the year.

Do you agree with how Ms. Clark handled the situation? If not, what could she have done differently?

COMMON MISCONCEPTIONS

Misconception 1: Building students' sense of belonging isn't really part of restorative practices.

Fact: For students to invest in the personal work of restorative conversations, circles, and conferences and to make the effort to change behaviors, actions, or perspectives, they need to feel a sense of belonging, acceptance, and commitment to the school and the people in it. Without a sense of belonging, students are more likely to withdraw from academics and the social aspects of school entirely.

Misconception 2: Students will automatically feel a sense of belonging and agency when the school has a written mission statement that commits to creating a welcoming atmosphere. These feelings are especially strengthened if that mission statement is posted on the wall in the main office.

Fact: Just because something is written and even posted on a wall doesn't mean the culture and climate of a school automatically reflect those values. Creating a sense of belonging and agency comes from all aspects of school—what's written on the walls around campus, how the teachers and staff interact with students, how positive and problematic behavior is addressed, how students are celebrated for success, how families are treated, and how students are empowered to make decisions.

Misconception 3: Words of encouragement are the best way to help students feel a sense of agency at school.

Fact: The language we use with, around, and about students is extremely important. However, time and attention are also key to students' sense of belonging and agency. Although it's important to set boundaries for your own mental and physical health, being accessible and investing your time in students shows them how much you care about their academic success and their development as people.

Misconception 4: "My credibility as a teacher is based on my subject knowledge. Because I know a lot, I convey my credibility to my students."

Fact: Your subject matter knowledge is only one aspect of teacher credibility. And when it comes to credibility, we don't get to decide— they do.

LEARNING INTENTIONS

- I am learning about how belongingness is linked to a restorative culture.

- I am learning about teacher credibility as a major influence on student learning.

- I am learning about investing in student agency to foster academic and social-emotional learning.

SUCCESS CRITERIA

- I can assess my practice as a contributor to a foundation of success.

- I can reflect on my efforts toward establishing and building credibility with my students.

- I can analyze opportunities for student agency in my classroom and school.

We titled this module "Foundations of Respect" because creating a respectful learning environment is crucial if students are going to learn. When students feel unsafe or afraid to take risks or be vulnerable, learning is hindered. And remember, we believe that students need to learn social, emotional, behavioral, and academic skills from their teachers. When educators foster a safe learning space, develop healthy growth-producing relationships with students, maintain their credibility, and build student agency, amazing things happen. And it starts with all students feeling that they belong in the learning environment.

WHEN EDUCATORS FOSTER A SAFE LEARNING SPACE, DEVELOP HEALTHY GROWTH-PRODUCING RELATIONSHIPS WITH STUDENTS, MAINTAIN THEIR CREDIBILITY, AND BUILD STUDENT AGENCY, AMAZING THINGS HAPPEN.

Goodenow (1993) defines belonging as being accepted, valued, included, and encouraged by others (teachers and peers) in the academic classroom and of feeling oneself to be an important part of the life and activity of the class. Belonging is a lever that promotes success, engagement, and well-being. As you will note in the self-assessment on page 32, there are a number of ways that a sense of belonging can be promoted or harmed.

Let's personalize this a bit more. Consider a learning time in your life when you did not feel that you belonged. What were your thoughts and actions? Now consider a time in your learning life when you felt that you belonged. Were your thoughts and actions different? How about the outcomes from those learning experiences? You probably noticed that when you felt a sense of belonging, you learned more and you felt better about the experience.

You may have noticed that belonging was not just your relationship with the teacher. We'll turn our attention to teacher-student relationships shortly. But belonging involves the whole class. When a student belongs, they experience acceptance, attention, and support from their peers as well as teachers. In other words, it's the emotional climate and structures that the teacher puts into place that create a sense of belonging. Figure 2.1 contains factors that Whiting et al. (2018) identified as contributing to a sense of belonging. They used exploratory and confirmatory factor analysis to identify these items and noted that they fell into four categories that educators may want to consider as they create belonging in classrooms and schools. They note that some of these were stronger than others, but they give us pause as we think about students' experiences in our classrooms and schools. These include

Factor 1: **School belonging**, or the feeling that a student feels comfortable, accepted, and liked at the school

Factor 2: **Feelings of rejection**, or the belief that who you are as a person is not valued

Factor 3: **Connection to teachers**, or the relatedness that students experience with the adults in the school

Factor 4: **School loyalty,** or the support students have for the school they attend

IT'S THE EMOTIONAL CLIMATE AND STRUCTURES THAT THE TEACHER PUTS INTO PLACE THAT CREATE A SENSE OF BELONGING.

Figure 2.1 Measuring Student Belonging

I feel like a real part of (school name).

People here notice when I am good at something.

It is hard for people like me to be accepted here.

Other students in this school take my opinions seriously.

Most teachers at this school are interested in me.

Sometimes I don't feel as if I belong here.

There's at least one teacher or adult in this school who I can talk to if I have a problem.

People at this school are friendly to me.

Teachers here are not interested in people like me.

I am included in lots of activities at this school.

I am treated with as much respect as other students.

I feel very different from most other students here.

I can really be myself at this school.

The teachers here respect me.

People here know that I can do good work.

I wish I were in a different school.

I feel proud of belonging to (school name).

(Continued)

(Continued)

Other students here like me the way I am.

I feel loyal to people in (school name).

I feel like I belong to (school name).

I would be willing to work together with others on something to improve (school name).

I like to think of myself as similar to others at (school name).

People at (school name) care if I am absent.

I fit in with other students at (school name).

I participate in activities at (school name).

I feel out of place at (school name).

I feel like my ideas count at (school name).

(School name) is a comfortable place for me.

I feel like I matter to people at (school name).

People really listen to me when I am at school.

Source: Whiting et al. (2018).

SELF-ASSESSMENT

Directions: Reflect on your current classroom environment. What is firmly in place? What do you want to strengthen?

CONDITION	IN PLACE	PARTIALLY IN PLACE	NOT IN PLACE
Communicate high expectations and your belief that all students can succeed.			
Learn and use students' names and identified pronouns (if they share them with you).			
Build rapport in the class through regular icebreakers, small group activities, collaborative thinking, etc.			
Develop guidelines or community agreements about interactions during class.			
Assess students' prior knowledge to align instruction with their strengths/needs.			

CONDITION	IN PLACE	PARTIALLY IN PLACE	NOT IN PLACE
Communicate concern for your students' well-being, and share information about school resources (e.g., sports, counseling, arts, clubs).			
Allow for productive trial and error (e.g., through low-stakes practice quizzes, drafting opportunities, modeling, or discussing interestingly productive wrong answers). Emphasize that risk, struggle, and failure can be important parts of any learning process and/or scientific method.			
Deliberately avoid generalizations that may exclude students who are already experiencing marginalization. These are often communicated through phrases that make implicit assumptions about students' physical ability, family structure, social identities, citizenship status, or economic means.			
Design policies that provide clear pathways if students need to be absent, turn in work late, leave class early, etc.			
Highlight the diversity of contributors to your discipline (through the authors you assign, the research you highlight, the guests you invite to meet with your students, etc.), and/or facilitate a discussion about the reasons for a history of limited access to the field and current efforts to change it.			
When possible, assign student groups or provide criteria for student-formed groups/teams that help leverage diversity and avoid isolating students from underrepresented identities.			
At the beginning of group work, create a process for students to discuss their respective strengths, personal learning goals, anticipated contributions, etc.			
Create intentional opportunities for students to provide feedback on their learning environment experience and share ideas for improving it. This assessment could include short anonymous polls, check-ins at the beginning of class, or more substantial written feedback opportunities.			

(Continued)

(Continued)

What other ways do I help facilitate my students' sense of belonging in my class? What else could I do? What are my next steps?

What can I do *this week* to make it more inclusive to help facilitate my students' sense of belonging?

Source: Adapted from Iowa State University, Center for Excellence in Learning and Teaching (2021). https://www.celt.iastate.edu/wp-content/uploads/2021/07/sense-of-belonging-practices.pdf

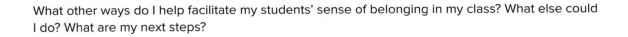

TEACHER CREDIBILITY

We have noted the importance of teacher-student relationships several times in this book and will continue to do so in nearly every module. Restorative practices rest on the development, maintenance, and repair of relationships. Teachers and students should have healthy, growth-producing relationships, in part because students learn more when these are present. Teacher-student relationships are part of a much larger system that operates in the classroom and that is teacher credibility. The question is: *Do your students believe that they can learn from you?* If your answer is yes, they will likely learn a lot more. And if the answer is yes, they are much more likely to act in ways that are consistent with the class agreements. Teacher credibility is more than the relationships that exist and specifically include trust, competence, dynamism or passion, and immediacy or perceived closeness.

TRUST

Students need to know that their teachers really care about them as individuals and have their best academic and social interests at heart. Students also want to know that their teachers are true to their word and are reliable. A few points about trust:

1. If you make a promise, work to keep it (or explain why you could not).

2. Tell students the truth about their performance (they know when their work is below standard and wonder why you are telling them otherwise).

3. Don't spend all your time trying to catch students in the wrong (and yet be honest about the impact that their behavior has on you as an individual).

4. Examine any negative feelings you have about specific students (they sense these feelings, and they compromise the trust within the classroom).

COMPETENCE

In addition to trust, students want to know that their teachers know their stuff and know how to teach that stuff. They expect an appropriate level of expertise and accuracy from their teachers. Further, students measure competence by the ability of the teacher to deliver instruction that is coherent and organized. They expect that lessons are well-paced, and the information is accurate.

1. Make sure you know the content well and be honest when a question arises that you are not sure about (this requires planning in advance).

2. Organize lesson delivery in a cohesive and coherent way.

3. Consider your nonverbal behaviors that communicate competence, such as the position of your hands when you talk with students or the facial expressions you make (students notice defensive positions and nonverbal indications that they are not valued when they speak).

DO YOUR STUDENTS BELIEVE THAT THEY CAN LEARN FROM YOU? IF YOUR ANSWER IS YES, THEY WILL LIKELY LEARN A LOT MORE.

DYNAMISM

This dimension of teacher credibility focuses on the passion teachers bring to the classroom and their content. It is really about your ability to communicate enthusiasm for your subject and your students. And it's about developing spirited lessons that capture students' interest. To improve dynamism,

1. **Rekindle your passion for the content you teach** by focusing on the aspects that got you excited as a student. Remember why you wanted to be a teacher and the content you wanted to introduce to your students. Revisit your reflections on this very topic from

Module 1! Now ask whether your students know why you became an educator. Students notice when their teachers are bored by the content and when their teachers aren't really interested in the topic. We think that a teacher's motto should be "Make content interesting!"

2. **Consider the relevance of your lessons.** Does the content lend itself to application outside the classroom? Do students have opportunities to learn about themselves and their problem solving? Does the content help them become civic-minded and engaged in their school and neighborhood community? Does it connect to universal human experiences, or ask students to grapple with ethical concerns? When there isn't relevance, students check out, reduced to being compliant learners rather than committed learners.

3. **Seek feedback from trusted colleagues about your lesson delivery.** Ask peers to sit in on a lesson to focus on the energy you bring and the impact on students' demeanors, rather than the individual instructional strategies you use. Students respond to the passion and energy in a lesson, even if they didn't initially think they would be interested.

> STUDENT AGENCY IS, IN PART, THE RECOGNITION THAT EFFORT AND OUTCOMES ARE RELATED.

Wangberg (1996) notes that "the best teachers are people who are passionate about their subject *and* passionate about sharing that subject with others" (p. 199).

IMMEDIACY

This final construct of teacher credibility focuses on accessibility and relatability as perceived by students. The concept of immediacy was introduced by social psychologist Albert Mehrabian (1971) who noted that "people are drawn toward persons and things they like, evaluate highly, and prefer; and they avoid or move away from things they dislike, evaluate negatively, or do not prefer" (p. 1). Teachers who move around the room and are easy to interact with increase students' perception of immediacy.

Teachers need to be accessible and yet there needs to be a sense of urgency that signals to students that their learning is important to you.

1. Get to know something personal about each student; students know when you don't know their names or anything about them.

2. Teach with urgency, but not to the point that it causes undue stress for them. That said, students want to know that their learning matters and that you are not wasting their time.

3. Start the class on time and use every minute wisely. This means that there are tasks students can complete while you engage in routine tasks such as taking attendance and that you have a series of sponge activities ready when lessons run short. Students notice when time is wasted. And when there is "free time," they believe that their learning is not an urgent consideration of their teachers.

Consider the following examples of general things you can do to ensure that your students feel close to you:

- Gesture when talking.

- Look at students and smile while talking.

- Call students by name.

- Use "we" and "us" to refer to the class.

- Invite students to provide feedback.

- Use vocal variety (pauses, inflections, stress, emphasis) when talking to the class.

Consider the following questions about your experiences with teacher credibility. How do you ensure that your students see you as credible?

1. How have I established trust with my students?

2. How do I demonstrate competence to my students?

3. How do I display my dynamism to my students?

4. How do I ensure that my students feel close to me?

5. What are my next steps in developing and maintaining my credibility?

BUILDING STUDENT AGENCY

Agency is central to a positive relationship to learning. As the OECD notes, "Student agency for 2030 is rooted in the belief that students have the ability and the will to influence positively their own lives and the world around them. Student agency is defined as the capacity to set a goal, reflect and act responsibly to effect change" (OECD, n.d.).

Student agency is, in part, the recognition that effort and outcomes are related. Students with low levels of agency believe that learning is something that happens to them, and if they don't learn something, it is because of the teacher's inadequacies, or their own traits. They don't see their own role in their learning. Student agency is multidimensional and fostered by approaches to instruction, task design, motivation, assessment, and the development of study habits. Research on student agency in schools identified eight dimensions: self-efficacy, pursuit of interest, perseverance of effort, locus of control, mastery orientation, metacognition, self-regulation, and future orientation (Zeiser et al., 2018).

STUDENTS DESERVE TO KNOW THAT WHEN THEY PUT FORTH EFFORT, CHANGE CAN HAPPEN.

We have explored student agency in other books (e.g., Fisher et al., 2021), so we will limit the conversation here to *connecting effort with outcomes*, especially when it comes to behavior. Building agency requires a shift in the language we use with students. We attribute success to their efforts. We specifically and intentionally make the connections between what they did and the good things that happened as a result. This is part of the foundation of respect, as students need to see that what they do matters. Students deserve to know that when they put forth effort, change can happen. Sometimes, with some students, we need to focus on the small wins. It may be too much to expect perfect behavior for an entire day at the outset, but putting practices in place to recognize the effort and the results can build the stamina of our students.

Notice the language that Ari's teacher uses in their conference. They are sitting at the back of their third-grade classroom and the rest of the class is working on a project. Jeremy Brown starts by greeting Ari.

"Ari, I'm so pleased that we could spend a few minutes together. I wanted to let you know that I noticed some things. First, I noticed that you took some breaths when you got frustrated with Ellis. And then you were able to let Ellis know what you needed. I bet that felt really good."

Ari responds, "Yeah, I got mad. But I didn't do anything bad. I did my strategy."

Mr. Brown: "You sure did. And it really seemed to work. I also noticed that you made a mistake, and I noticed that it was okay with you. You didn't get frustrated. You said that you made a mistake, and you asked for help. You know how much I like mistakes because they help us learn. And you did it. You made a mistake and learned more. I also noticed that you, Ari, used some tools when you got a little distracted. You did that, and it also seemed to work. Do you agree?"

"For sure. I had a good class today, and it wasn't really that hard. I just need to remember my strategies. I also have friends here who can remind me. But I did it today by myself. I didn't need them."

In this brief exchange, Mr. Brown is attributing Ari's success to the actions and decisions taken. Mr. Brown is also providing Ari with an opportunity to reflect on those successes and the specific things that we have done to create those successes.

BUILD STUDENT AGENCY WITH INTENTION

Invitational teaching is intentional teaching. To build student agency, a crucial factor in self-regulation and academic success, engage in these five practices. These are derived from two years of work by the American Institutes for Research, in collaboration with four high schools.

Relationships. Positive student-teacher relationships promote student motivation for learning and are more than just being pleasant with students. By forming bonds with students, we encourage them to value themselves, others, and their learning.

Feedback. Well known as an influencer and accelerator of learning, the feedback research is often misinterpreted. With an effect size of 0.62, feedback is an established part of learning, whether for academic, social, or behavioral purposes (www.visiblelearningmetax.com). The misconception? This is about feedback *received*, not feedback *given*. When the source of the feedback is not credible, and there is little relationship to the source, feedback is ignored. It's feedback that is acted upon that is the game-changer.

Goal setting. Feedback paired with the establishment and monitoring of one's goals is especially powerful. A student with a deep motivation and goal-oriented approach seeks mastery and is willing to invest a higher degree of effort. That kind of motivation has an effect size of 0.57 and can accelerate learning (Hattie, n.d.; www.visiblelearningmetax.com), which is why we encourage conversations with students about their goals.

Individual conferences. Meet with students on a regular basis to discuss their learning. A goal is to encourage them to think metacognitively, which is to say reflectively. Often described as "thinking about thinking," metacognition develops in the first years of schooling and continues across a lifetime. Much like the individual conference Mr. Brown had with Ari, these are ideal occasions to link their efforts to their results.

Student voice. Agency can't develop when there are few opportunities to make choices and decisions about their learning and about their classroom. Vaughn et al. (2020) found that elementary students with a strong sense of agency answered positively to items such as "My teacher asks for our opinions to decide what to do" and "We share our thoughts and our teacher acts on them."

INDIVIDUAL REFLECTION

Use the traffic light scale to reflect on your current practices as they relate to teaching about and creating opportunities for agency. What areas do you want to strengthen?

STUDENT–TEACHER COLLABORATION

Developing relationships. Teachers develop personal relationships with students to better understand their agency strengths, needs, and motivators.	
Feedback. Teachers provide students with feedback and scaffold the process of students seeking feedback.	
Goal setting. Teachers help students set goals to complete coursework while improving agency.	
Individual conferences. Teachers hold one-on-one meetings with students to discuss elements of student agency and its relationship to academic work.	
Student voice. Teachers provide students with opportunities to contribute to and provide feedback on key decisions in the classroom.	

Source: Excerpted from Zeiser et al. (2018).

WEAVING A CULTURE OF BELONGING AND AGENCY DEVELOPMENT INTO THE SCHOOL DAY

School culture is built by *what you do* throughout campus. School climate is *how you feel* while at school. To help students feel a culture of belonging and develop their agency, it is important to consider what we do at key touchpoints in the school year as well as in our daily practices.

The first touchpoint to consider is the opening of the school year or a new semester. Think about how you greet students and make them feel special the moment they step on campus on the first day of school. Are there balloons, music, and a welcome committee of teachers and staff out front to say hello and greet students as they enter the building/school grounds? Do you put up a VIP sign in front of your door and greet each student personally as they walk into your room for the first time?

Another way to help students develop belongingness is to spend time throughout the year engaging in team-building activities. The goal is for students to not only feel that they belong in your class but that they belong to the school as a whole—that they are part of something bigger than just themselves. While these are often done during the first week of school, they are rapidly forgotten when they are perceived as one-off activities. Select days throughout the year that are dedicated to team building.

The second touchpoint to help build students' sense of belonging is to consider how students experience a return from an absence or come late to school. While this occurrence happens often throughout the school year, each time is an important opportunity to rebuild a student's sense of belonging to the school/classroom community. For example, when a student arrives late, the front office staff can use language such as, "So good to see you! How was your morning so far? What happened to make you late today?" Warmly inviting the student into the building opens the opportunity for discussion rather than makes them feel guilty for being late—which, for many students, especially young children, may be out of their control. Additionally, instead of "Here's what you missed yesterday," consider language that welcomes the student back to the classroom such as "We missed you. It's so good to have you back! Our classroom isn't the same without you. Let's plan to talk a little later so that I can bring you up to speed."

SCHOOL CULTURE IS BUILT BY *WHAT YOU DO* THROUGHOUT CAMPUS. SCHOOL CLIMATE IS *HOW YOU FEEL* WHILE AT SCHOOL.

The third touchpoint is in ensuring that students have ownership in their classroom and school. This is an investment in intentional ways student agency is fostered more broadly. Student decision making about school matters. Student empowerment means that we might need to shift our thinking about how we partner with them in consequential ways. The first step is to gauge the current status of student empowerment at your school. Begin by cataloging the ways students are currently involved in school and community matters. You may discover that there are higher levels of community empowerment after school than during the school day. Once current opportunities have been identified, evaluate each based on the degree of meaningful involvement. Figure 2.2 has a list of possible ways to increase student involvement in school.

Figure 2.2 Student Empowerment Opportunities

ELEMENTARY SCHOOLS

- Membership in a school improvement committee
- Co-constructed curricular units reflecting student interests
- Student-led family conferences
- Student classroom governance (e.g., class meetings)
- Student jobs in the front office, in the library, on the safety patrol, or as school ambassadors
- Student-led signature campaigns on civic engagement issues

MIDDLE SCHOOLS

- Membership in all school committees
- Co-teaching
- Co-design and implementation of whole-school forums
- Service learning for the school community
- Agenda items for a school improvement committee submitted by students

HIGH SCHOOLS

- Student representation on district committees, including budget committees
- Co-planning on course design
- Participation in professional development
- Membership in professional learning communities
- Positions on teacher- and school leader–hiring teams
- Design and implementation of whole-school forums about school and community issues
- Student-led educational conferences

Source: Adapted from Fletcher (2005).

A DILEMMA: TAKE TWO

Students' names are an important part of the beginning of the year. When we don't spend time learning how to pronounce students' names correctly, we send the message that we don't see them, we don't want to really know them, and they don't belong. Think about Ms. Clark's classroom. She spent so much time preparing activities with the intent to build a sense of belonging in her classroom, but when it came to pronouncing Arundhathi's name correctly, Ms. Clark let her own embarrassment and discomfort get in the way of valuing the student's identity.

Ms. Clark notices in the week that followed that "Dottie" doesn't love this name. She speaks with another colleague who had Arundhathi's older sister, Subalakshmi, in his class. Mr. Sanders agrees that the girls' names were challenging because they were unfamiliar to them, but that they were common in other places and an important part of their cultural and personal identities. He shares how he was improving his pronunciation by asking Subalakshmi for feedback.

Ms. Clark takes his advice and meets with Arundhathi the next day. "Wow! You have a unique and special name. I wanted to learn more about it, and I found out that it means 'washed from the rays of the sun.' That's a really beautiful picture in my mind. My first name is Dawn, and that has a sun meaning, too," she says. "Do you know how you got your name?"

Arundhathi brightens up and tells her teacher that in Indian culture it is traditional for parents to meet with an astrologer to find out the sound a child's name should begin with, and then the parents choose a name that starts with the same sound.

Ms. Clark says, "I had no idea. And I want to apologize for asking you to take a nickname because I was uncomfortable. Clearly, I'm having a hard time saying it correctly right now. But I promise I am going to keep practicing because it's important to me that I get it right. When you hear me say it wrong in the future, please correct me."

Arundhathi, wise beyond her years, says, "'Cause that's what good teachers do. They help people learn."

THE GOAL IS FOR STUDENTS TO NOT ONLY FEEL THAT THEY BELONG IN YOUR CLASS BUT THAT THEY BELONG TO THE SCHOOL AS A WHOLE—THAT THEY ARE PART OF SOMETHING BIGGER THAN JUST THEMSELVES.

CASE IN POINT

The Abadis are a military family. They have just been transferred to a new area and enrolled their three children in the local public schools. Their oldest son, Khalil, is in middle school. He is used to being "the new kid" because of his dad's military status. But being "the new kid" and "the Muslim kid" at school is often hard for him. He is feeling a bit nervous about his first day of school, especially because it's the middle of the school year and he knows that all the social cliques are well established by now.

When he walks into the office on his first day to get his schedule, he is surprised to see the principal and two students from his grade waiting for him. They all introduce themselves and the principal explains that the students will be giving Khalil a tour of the school to make sure he knows where all his classes are, as well as the main common areas on campus.

When Khalil returns from the tour, the principal walks him to a third-period class (not the section he will join, but the same subject) and tells him to sit in the back of the room to observe and take notes about how the class is run. She wants him to do the same for a fourth-period class. The principal explains that after class she'd like him to come back to her office and share his observations with her, specifically what he sees that is different than his previous school and what is similar.

STUDENT DECISION MAKING ABOUT SCHOOL MATTERS.

At lunch, Khalil gets the opportunity to eat with several of his teachers. They are meeting him for the first time as a person, as he has not yet attended their classes. He feels a little awkward sitting with a bunch of adults, but it's nice to meet them all in a relaxed setting and have time to get to know each other.

After school, when Khalil's mom picks him up, he can't stop talking about how great the school is and how he is looking forward to the next day. She is pleasantly surprised at how excited he seems.

What practices did the school engage in to help Khalil feel welcome as a new student? Are there any improvements they could have made?

RECOMMENDATIONS AND IMPLICATIONS

We have created a table of general recommendations for consideration. Add your own site-specific implications and questions that this module has provoked for you.

	BROAD RECOMMENDATIONS	SITE-SPECIFIC IMPLICATIONS AND QUESTIONS
Schoolwide	Gauge the current level of student belonging and agency at the school. What efforts support or detract from these outcomes?	
Leaders	Learn from teachers about how they foster belonging and agency in their classrooms and spotlight ideas with the staff.	
Teachers	Examine how you are credible with your students and identify areas of strength and growth opportunities.	
Students	Teach students about agency and link this to activities and processes in the classroom.	
Family and Community	Invite families and community leaders to discuss their sense of belonging in the school and ask for ways to improve it.	

REFLECTION

Let's review the success criteria from the opening of this module. Ask yourself: Can you do these things now? Write your reflections below.

Can I assess my practice as a contributor to a foundation of success?	
Can I reflect on my efforts toward establishing and building credibility with my students?	
Can I analyze opportunities for student agency in my classroom and school?	

Access resources, tools, and guides
for this module at the companion website:
resources.corwin.com/restorativepracticesplaybook

Module 3

ESTABLISHING EXPECTATIONS AND TEACHING FOR ENGAGEMENT

BELIEF STATEMENT

When students understand the expectations of their learning environment, they are more likely to make decisions and take actions that are consistent with the agreements they have made.

A Dilemma

Lisa Patton is looking forward to meeting her new students. The start of a school year is always an exciting time, and Ms. Patton wants to start the year with clear expectations for her second graders. Ms. Patton has purchased a poster from her local teacher store with a list of classroom rules that include some specifics ("Raise your hand before speaking.") and some general guidelines ("Let's all do our best!"). Ms. Patton also has her clip chart ready and strategically places it to the left of her smartboard.

On the first day of school, Ms. Patton introduces students to the classroom rules and provides each student a copy for their notebooks. The students are asked to share examples highlighting when they are and are not following the rules. Ms. Patton then focuses on her clip chart. She informs students that they will move their clips up or down along the chart based on their behaviors in the classroom. If they get all the way to the bottom of the chart, she will contact parents or family members.

Later that same day, Mari and Jaime are talking. A lot. And they won't stop. Ms. Patton stops the lesson and tells both students to move their clip to red and that she will be contacting their families that night. Jaime starts crying but walks to the board and moves the clip. Mari refuses to move from her seat.

Is there another way to establish classroom procedures that might prevent these situations?

COMMON MISCONCEPTIONS

"Is academic rigor the enemy of restorative practices?" That question was posed to us by a district director of curriculum and instruction, who was wrestling with how their existing initiative on high expectations might be undermined by anticipated work on restorative practices. The director's hesitation is echoed in the teacher's dilemma you just read. Ms. Patton wants to make sure she is holding her students to high expectations. Or is she? We'd like to address some misconceptions before going deeper into this module.

Misconception 1: Restorative practices are mostly confined to dimensions of social-emotional learning. They don't really inform academic learning.

Fact: Academic learning is directly impacted by the social-emotional skills of the student. It has been well-documented that the noncognitive skills of motivation, self-regulation, prosocial skills, problem solving, and clear communication impact student learning.

Misconception 2: The standards and curricular frameworks communicate the expectations we have for all students.

Fact: Teacher expectations of individual students are highly predictive of their academic learning. These expectations also vary based on teachers' experiences, bias, and student demographics. These expectations are also influenced by the behavior of students. Developing students' social and behavioral skills allows them to access rigorous content and respond to high-quality instruction.

Misconception 3: Student engagement is essential for learning and requires high levels of teacher control to properly manage the classroom.

Fact: Students in classrooms with high levels of teacher control grow to dislike school as the year progresses, whether they are rewarded frequently or infrequently. Their family's relationship with the school also declines (Kowalski & Froiland, 2020).

Misconception 4: Teachers are responsible for establishing and enforcing classroom rules.

Fact: Emotional supports, classroom organization, and instructional supports are positively impacted by the practice of co-constructing class agreements with students. These foster a shared responsibility for enacting them.

MODULE 3

LEARNING INTENTIONS

- I am learning about teacher expectations and students' learning.
- I am learning about engagement and the reasons that students disengage.

SUCCESS CRITERIA

- I can identify actions that communicate high expectations for students.
- I can describe engagement across a continuum and develop lessons to teach students about engagement.
- I can identify reasons that students disengage and implement actions that invite them back into learning.
- I can implement a process for developing classroom agreements and revisit these as needed.

AN INVITATION TO LEARN IN A RESTORATIVE CULTURE

There is an adage that suggests it is the teacher who sets the weather in the classroom. This is borne out in the extensive research about the psychosocial climate for learning, particularly in students' perceptions of the emotional and instructional support they receive in the classroom (Hamre et al., 2013). You have undoubtedly experienced this same phenomenon in your own educational career, whether student or teacher. There are some classrooms that feel instantly inviting, while others do not. We're not talking about how the room is decorated, although the physical environment can contribute to the overall culture of learning. It's something less tangible—is it a perception? Or is there more to it?

IT IS THE TEACHER WHO SETS THE WEATHER IN THE CLASSROOM.

The notion of invitational teaching was forwarded by Purkey and Novak in 1996, and it continues to resonate today. They described invitational teaching through four lenses:

- **Trust.** Trust is defined as the ongoing relationships between the teacher and students. In trusting classrooms, teachers and students assume positive intentions and seek to build, maintain, and repair those relationships.

- **Respect.** This condition is fostered through actions that communicate an understanding of everyone's autonomy, identity, and value to the learning community. Shared responsibility is crucial, and members of the classroom, including the teacher, see themselves as stewards for maintaining the social and emotional well-being of others.

- **Optimism.** The potential of each classroom member is untapped, and every member of the classroom is responsible for finding ways to help others reach their potential. Teachers are important in creating optimistic learning environments, and so are students. In an inviting classroom, students support the learning of their peers and understand that they are key in others' learning. Purkey and Novak believe that a life without hope impairs a person's ability to move forward. If schools are not places to find hope, then what use are they?

- **Intentionality.** An invitation to learning means that the practices, policies, processes, and programs of classrooms and schools are carefully designed to convey trust, respect, and optimism to all.

Having said that, these may not be evidenced in reality. It's more than just saying "All children can learn." The researchers took two of those conditions—intention and invitation—and discussed four possible types of teachers (see Figure 3.1).

Figure 3.1 Four Types of Teachers

Intentionally uninviting teachers . . .	Intentionally inviting teachers . . .
Are judgmental and belittling	Are consistent and steady with students
Display little care or regard	Notice learning and struggle
Are uninterested in the lives and feelings of students	Respond regularly with feedback
Isolate themselves from school life	Seek to build, maintain, and repair relationships
Seek power over students	
Unintentionally uninviting teachers . . .	**Unintentionally inviting teachers . . .**
Distance themselves from students	Are eager but unreflective
Have low expectations	Are energetic but rigid when facing problems
Don't feel effective, and blame students for shortcomings	Are unaware of what works in their practice, and why
Fail to notice student learning or struggle	Have fewer means for responding when student learning is resistant to their usual methods
Offer little feedback to learners	

Source: Adapted from Purkey & Novak (1996).

Directions: How might students react to each of these conditions? List behaviors and other signs to watch for in each of these classrooms.

STUDENTS WITH INTENTIONALLY UNINVITING TEACHERS MIGHT DO/SAY . . .	STUDENTS WITH INTENTIONALLY INVITING TEACHERS MIGHT DO/SAY . . .
STUDENTS WITH UNINTENTIONALLY UNINVITING TEACHERS MIGHT DO/SAY . . .	STUDENTS WITH UNINTENTIONALLY INVITING TEACHERS MIGHT DO/SAY . . .

HIGH EXPECTATIONS IN A RESTORATIVE CULTURE

The expectations of teachers are communicated to students verbally and nonverbally. The blatant verbal ones are more easily controlled—most of us are able to avoid obvious statements (*"You're stupid not to know this by now"*).

Babad (1998) led investigations of classrooms and compared them to teachers' perceptions of their practice. She noted that teachers reported that they lent more emotional support to students who struggled. In her book on high expectation teachers, Rubie-Davies (2014) described these observations:

> This is not to say that low expectation students received negative emotional support. On the contrary, Babad reported that teachers did endeavor to display warmth and emotional support towards low expectation students. Students were able, however, to determine that such displays were not genuine, because they were exaggerated, whereas teachers' natural affection for the high expectation students was interpretable by students, despite teacher attempts to control this. (pp. 152–153)

Low expectation students, the research concluded, resented the uneven distribution of emotional support in the classroom, sometimes identifying the high expectation students as "the teacher's pet." Given that, peer relationships in the classroom are strongly influenced by the relationship the teacher has with an individual student. In fact, most students are readily able to identify who the teacher likes and doesn't like. But we rarely ask that question because the answer is uncomfortable.

MOST OF US HAVE NOT DIRECTLY TAUGHT STUDENTS WHAT IT MEANS TO ENGAGE.

The expectations are communicated in the instruction we use, the way we group students, and even in the use of formative assessments to inform learning. Taking the decades of research on teacher expectations, Rubie-Davies (2015) transformed the findings from these many studies by linking them to specific organizational decisions teachers make every day. What is especially striking are the findings on how expectations influence planning; in other words, what occurs before we ever set foot in the classroom? Teachers who have high expectations believe that the students they teach will make accelerated growth, not simply "normal" progress (Rubie-Davies, 2014). Teachers with lower expectations assign tasks that are less cognitively demanding, spend time repeating information over and over again, focus on classroom rules and procedures, and accept a lower standard of work. High expectation teachers in mixed ability classrooms don't differentiate the *learning*. All students learn complex content, which is not always the case for some students. The evidence is that students perceived by their teacher as being of low ability do far more work around procedures, discrete skills, and are asked low-level questions. High expectation teachers, on the other hand, provide a range of learning tasks designed to support the attainment of grade-level goals. They differentiate the *tasks*, not the learning.

MODULE 3

SELF-ASSESSMENT: ARE YOU A HIGH EXPECTATION TEACHER?

Directions: Use the following self-assessment checklist to identify the frequency of the high expectation practices that you use.

HOW OFTEN DO YOU USE THE FOLLOWING HIGH EXPECTATION PRACTICES IN YOUR TEACHING?	RARELY	SOMETIMES	OFTEN
Ask open questions.			
Praise effort rather than correct answers.			
Use regular formative assessment.			
Rephrase questions when answers are incorrect.			
Use mixed ability groupings.			
Change groupings regularly.			
Encourage students to work with a range of their peers.			
Provide a range of activities.			
Allow students to choose their own activities from a range of options.			
Make explicit learning intentions and success criteria.			
Allow students to contribute to success criteria.			
Give students responsibility for their learning.			
Get to know each student personally.			
Incorporate students' interests into activities.			
Establish routines and procedures at the beginning of the school year.			
Work with students to set individual goals.			
Teach students about SMART (specific, measurable, achievable, relevant, and time-bound) goals.			
Regularly review goals with students.			
Link achievement to motivation, effort, and goal setting.			
Minimize differentiation in activities between high and low achievers.			

HOW OFTEN DO YOU USE THE FOLLOWING HIGH EXPECTATION PRACTICES IN YOUR TEACHING?	RARELY	SOMETIMES	OFTEN
Allow all learners to engage in advanced activities.			
Give specific instructional feedback about students' achievement in relation to learning goals.			
Take a facilitative role and support students to make choices about their learning.			
Manage behavior positively and proactively.			
Work with all students equally.			

Source: Hargreaves (2018, https://theeducationhub.org.nz/high-expectations-self-assessment-checklist). Developed from Rubie-Davies (2014).

ENGAGEMENT IN A RESTORATIVE CULTURE

When students are not engaged, their learning is at risk. It's hard to learn when you are not paying attention or focused on the information at hand. And teachers become frustrated when their students are not engaged. In the past, engagement has been seen as a dichotomy: either students were or were not engaged. When a given student failed to engage, their teacher would typically bribe or punish them. The reality is that most of us have not directly taught students what it means to engage. Ask yourself these questions:

- Have I directly taught what is meant by engagement?
- Do I have students set their intention for engagement each day?
- Do have tools for students to monitor their engagement?
- Do I invite students to reflect on their engagement after a lesson?

More recent research suggests that engagement occurs along a continuum. Berry (2020) sought to develop a continuum of engagement that recognized that

1. Engagement can vary throughout a lesson.
2. There is a relationship between engagement, motivation, and learning.

Working with teachers, Berry developed a continuum of engagement that is more holistic and especially takes the degree of learning into account (see Figure 3.2).

Notice that learners are passive in the middle and become more active as they move to the right or left. In other words, students can be actively disengaged or actively engaged. Interestingly, moving to the right increases the amount of learning that students do.

Figure 3.2 A Continuum of Engagement

ACTIVE ⟵———————————— PASSIVE ————————————⟶ ACTIVE

Disrupting	Avoiding	Withdrawing	Participating	Investing	Driving
Distracting others Disrupting the learning environment	Looking for ways to avoid tasks Off-task behavior	Being mentally distracted Physically separating from the group or the work	Completing assigned tasks Focusing on the person speaking Responding to questions	Asking myself and others clarifying questions Feeling like what you are learning is important Body language conveys an interest in learning	Setting goals Seeking feedback Self-assessment

DISENGAGEMENT	ENGAGEMENT

Source: Adapted from the work of Berry (2020).

THE KEY TO THIS CONTINUUM IS TO TEACH IT TO STUDENTS.

The key to this continuum is to teach it to students. Don't simply copy the chart and place it on a wall. Instead, introduce the ideas and have students generate examples for each level of the continuum. In Marisa Diaz's kindergarten class, every student has a graphic/visual version of the continuum on their desk. They also have a small token that they move during the lesson as they monitor their engagement. Five-year-old Hector says, "Today, I am here [pointing to 'investing']. I was asking my questions. I was paying attention so that I can do my work. I didn't bother my friends when we were learning."

In Rick Marshall's biology class, students have defined each level of the continuum and set their intention each day at the start of class. Mr. Marshall's students reflect on their level of engagement, providing evidence, as part of their daily exit slip. As Naima says, "I set my goal to participate today. I'm not really feeling it, but I know that this content is important and that I am going to need to write an argument essay. So, I decided to participate. But then, it got really interesting when we were talking about animal experiments, and I actually moved to 'investing.' I started asking more questions and found myself more engaged. My evidence is that I asked three questions and I was leaning in the whole time, like I was really focused."

Of course, there are times when students acknowledge that they are not engaged. Kayla, a sixth grader, mentions, "I'm avoiding learning. I have a lot going on and I'm distracted, but I'm trying not to impact other people." Kayla's teacher notes, "I appreciated knowing that was where she was at. If I can get her to move a little bit, I can move her to withdrawing, and then it's not too far for her to start participating. Knowing this reduces my frustration and lets me set a goal for myself and my students. And then, we don't have so much conflict."

Now that you have been introduced to the engagement continuum, revisit the questions raised at the outset of this section. This time, take some notes about what you can do.

Have I directly taught what is meant by engagement?	
Do I have students set their intention for engagement each day?	
Do I have tools for students to monitor their engagement?	
Do I invite students to reflect on their engagement after a lesson?	

OVERCOMING COGNITIVE CHALLENGES TO LEARNING

Of course, there are times when students choose to disengage, as noted by Kayla. Chew and Cerbin (2020) described nine cognitive reasons that students do disengage. When we know these reasons, we can identify why a specific student has disengaged and then we can take action to re-engage that learner. It's empowering. As you review these cognitive challenges to learning, note that they do not only apply to children and youth. Think about your learning environments and when these might apply to you.

1. **Mental mindset.** The student approaches learning with a mindset that is not productive. That may be a belief about skills (as in "I'm not a good writer"), expected failure (as in "I failed math before and it will be the same this time"), or a lack of relevance for the learning.

2. **Metacognition and self-regulation.** The student does not yet engage in metacognitive skills, such as monitoring, questioning, or reflecting, which causes disengagement in learning. Or the student does not yet exhibit strong self-regulation skills such as focusing, re-directing attention, or perseverance.

3. **Fear and mistrust.** As the affective filter increases, learning decreases. This may be due to bullying, trauma, adverse childhood events, or a belief that the teacher is not fair. Regardless, the teacher-student relationship is not strong, and thus learning is compromised.

4. **Insufficient prior knowledge.** The learner lacks critical knowledge that is preventing the new learning from occurring. It's much easier to learn when going from the known to the new. Without sufficient prior knowledge, students may be lost in the new learning.

5. **Misconceptions.** All learners have misconceptions that impact their learning. And misconceptions tend to persist even when provided accurate information. Failure to recognize and address misconceptions results in less learning and students tend to disengage.

6. **Ineffective learning strategies.** The learner has a strategy to learn but realizes that it's not working and gives up. When students start a task but then stop, it's likely that they are not sure what to do when their learning strategies do not work in that situation.

7. **Transfer of learning.** The learner has the skills, knowledge, content, etc. but does not know how to use it. Teaching it again will not help because the issue lies in application, generalization, and transfer.

8. **Constraints of selective attention.** The myth of multitasking is real. We all believe that we are exceptions to the research, but our brains are not effective in completing multiple cognitive tasks at the same time. This distraction looks like disengagement, even though the student may not mean any harm (as they have likely seen many adults in their lives "multitasking").

9. **Constraints of mental effort and working memory.** At some point, learners reach cognitive overload. And when they do, they disengage from learning. In fact, they may even experience diminished returns and forget things if they are trying to concentrate on information that is too complex or if there is too much information.

In Figure 3.3, we offer a few ideas that you can use to address each of the nine cognitive challenges identified by Chew and Cerbin (2020). There are likely many more ideas that you can identify, individually and collaboratively. We invite you to identify the indicators that each challenge is occurring. For example, we noted that when students get started on a task or assignment and then quit, it may be due to ineffective learning strategies. When you become skilled at identifying these valid reasons for students' disengagement, you can take action to invite the student back into learning without relying on punishment and frustration.

Figure 3.3 Responses to Cognitive Challenges

CHALLENGE	INDICATORS	POTENTIAL ACTIONS
1. Mental mindset	• • •	• Explain the value and importance of the learning (relevance). • Increase students' ownership of their learning. • Teach habits of minds and mindsets. • •
2. Metacognition and self-regulation	• • •	• Create reflection assignments. • Teach students about planning, monitoring, and adjusting their learning. • Use practice tests. • •
3. Fear and mistrust	• • •	• Focus on trust between teachers and students. • Restructure feedback to ensure that students experience it as growth-producing. • Create a safe climate for learning and making mistakes. • •

(Continued)

(Continued)

CHALLENGE	INDICATORS	POTENTIAL ACTIONS
4. Insufficient prior knowledge	• • • • •	• Use initial assessments to identify what students already know and what they need to know. • Provide lesson background knowledge and key vocabulary in advance, perhaps through interactive videos. • Identify what students need to know versus what would be neat for them to know. • •
5. Misconceptions	• • •	• Use advance organizers that allow student misconceptions to surface. • Recognize common misconceptions for students at a specific age or in a specific content area. • Invite students to justify their responses to that thinking. • •
6. Ineffective learning strategies	• • •	• Teach study skills. • Model effective strategies with think-alouds. • Teach about and use spaced practice.
7. Transfer of learning	• • •	• Plan appropriate tasks that include near and far transfer. • Model the application of skills and concepts in different contexts. • Tailor feedback to include processing of the task. • •

CHALLENGE	INDICATORS	POTENTIAL ACTIONS
8. Constraints of selective attention	• • •	• Increase teacher clarity such that students know what they are learning and why. • Use breaks and re-orientation strategies. • Teach students to avoid multi-tasking, especially with media. • •
9. Constraints of mental effort and working memory	• • •	• Organize information and chunk it in ways that are easy to digest. • Use both visual and auditory cues (dual coding). • Use retrieval practice and universal response frequently. • •

Source: Adapted from Fisher & Frey (2021).

CLASS AGREEMENTS IN A RESTORATIVE CULTURE

At the beginning of this module, we noted the value of students agreeing on the ways in which their learning environment should operate (Adams & Bell, 2016). These class agreements, sometimes called class promises, can be co-constructed by the members of the class. Nancy likes to start with some general ideas for the group, as they broadly reflect her beliefs about learning:

- Take care of yourself.
- Take care of each other.
- Take care of this place.

From there, students can define and add to the agreements that will serve to organize the experiences they have. For example, in one high school class, students wanted practice tests. They said that they needed to practice before they were going to get a grade. Interestingly, the school focuses on competencies, and students are allowed to retake or redo assessments to improve their grades. The students understood that but wanted practice tests "so that we can take care of ourselves and not stress over getting an Incomplete and the need to clear that Incomplete if we don't pass the first time." That agreement was added to the list that also included the ways in which people would be addressed and the respect for one voice at a time, among others. We highlight this agreement because it was identified by students but had implications for the teacher, as the teacher would need to develop these practice tests to live up to the agreements in this class.

THE AGREEMENTS THAT STUDENTS WANT TO HAVE IN THEIR LEARNING ENVIRONMENT NEED TO REFLECT THE CURRENT REALITIES AND NOT THE PAST.

In an elementary classroom, one of the class agreements reads: "Try new things, even if they scare us." The conversation that led to this agreement was fascinating. The students in the class wanted to take risks but not be embarrassed if they failed at first. One of the students said, "In my old school when we tried things that were hard, other people in the class would tease you. Like if they did it fast and you didn't, they made fun of you." As their conversation continued, the teacher helped to shape the language of their agreement and asked for examples from students. Another student commented, "We should try because we are still learning. And if you already know it, you can help people but not tell them the answer or be mean to them because they are learning."

The blog "What Ed Said" has tips for creating class agreements (2014):

1. Don't start till you've spent some time establishing your own beliefs about learning.

2. Have the students consider what helps them learn and what hinders their learning.

3. Begin with what the learners value or the school values.

4. Have students unpack your school's learning principles as a starting point.

5. Base it on a common set of qualities, such as the International Baccalaureate® (IB) Learner Profile.

6. Use a placemat activity so students have time to think individually, before seeking consensus.

7. Have kids think about what learning looks like, sounds like, and feels like.

8. Take your time. Build the agreement gradually to ensure understanding and ownership.

9. Include photos and descriptions for younger learners, to elaborate on the words.

10. Live it, don't laminate it. Revisit the agreement often and adjust as required.

If you are not familiar with the placemat activity, it's a cooperative learning tool that allows students to think individually and then work with a small group to share ideas and work toward consensus. Students work in groups of three, four, or five. They have a piece of paper (larger is better) that has a dedicated space for each student and a central space for areas of agreement. They each record ideas in their own space and then have a conversation about what they have in common. Individuals can share their ideas and see if others want to adopt those ideas as well. This process ensures that there are many ideas that the small group and then the whole class can discuss. And many students find it safer to test their ideas with a small group and not the whole class at once.

Did you notice the final recommendation—that class agreements are revisited and can be revised? That's a very important point and one that is often forgotten. Things change and things happen and the agreements that students want to have in their learning environment need to reflect the current realities and not the past. For example, a group of fourth graders wanted to add an agreement based on some things that happened during recess. They settled on the language "Include people if they look excluded" following a discussion about a series of events that had impacted the group.

A DILEMMA: TAKE TWO

Ms. Patton reflects later in the day about the situation that occurred with two of her third-grade students. "Jaime was crying about moving her clip and Mari dug in her heels and withdrew psychologically from the class," says the teacher. "Here it was, the first day of school, and I had already shut down the learning of two children. That's not the learning environment I wanted to create."

Ms. Patton consults with another teacher who talked previously about setting a restorative culture in his classroom. "I told him what happened and asked him to advise me. What I really appreciated was that he didn't give me a list of things to do. Instead, he asked me some questions to mediate my own thinking." Among the questions her colleague, Jamal Turner, asks are these:

- "What are your core beliefs about learning?" ("That really got me thinking," she said.)

- "Why do you think this is right?"

- "What's your hunch about what happened?"

- "What are you most afraid might happen?"

- "What's the one thing you won't compromise?"

They talk for about 10 minutes, creating a space for Ms. Patton to think reflectively. When she asks again for advice, both she and Mr. Turner are much clearer about her expectations for herself and her students. He tells her how he sets up the discussions for class agreements during the first week of school and intersperses them with academic and social activities to allow him and his fifth graders to learn about one another. He shares information about invitational teaching and makes arrangements to talk with her again at the end of the week. The following day, Ms. Patton meets individually with Jamie and Mari, using affective statements (more on that in the next module) and then hosting a class circle (more on circles in Module 6). "I told them that in this classroom, everyone is a learner, including me. I introduced what class agreements are all about and began the conversation about what we want our classroom community to be."

Ms. Patton reflected that this isn't a one-and-done activity but rather their mutual investment in one another across the school year. "I've already put it on my calendar, when we're going to revisit our class agreements throughout the first quarter," she says. "Then we'll take it from there."

Now read the following scenario and consider what advice you have for the teacher and the school.

CASE IN POINT

Middle school teacher Mario Benavidez engages his students in discussions about class agreements. Each of his classes, six in total, develop their agreements. But Mr. Benavidez notes that they are different for each class, and he is worried that he might forget which ones apply to which classes. He also notes that some of his colleagues also had students develop class agreements and some did not. He wonders about the cumulative effect of having agreements in each class and if there should be some schoolwide agreements that might help create a healthy climate in the school.

> What advice do you have for Mr. Benavidez and the other teachers at the school?

RECOMMENDATIONS AND IMPLICATIONS

We have created a table of general recommendations for consideration. Add your own site-specific implications and questions that this module has provoked for you.

	BROAD RECOMMENDATIONS	SITE-SPECIFIC IMPLICATIONS AND QUESTIONS
Schoolwide	Learn about evidence-based practices about high expectations and engagement.	
Leaders	Assist teachers in taking an inventory of their high expectation behaviors and help them establish goals for themselves as growth opportunities.	
Teachers	Teach students about their definitions of engagement and its role in their learning.	
Students	Have students monitor their level of engagement regularly.	
Family and Community	Survey families about their engagement with the school to identify affordances and barriers.	

REFLECTION

Let's review the success criteria from the opening of this module. Ask yourself: Can you do these things now? Write your reflections below.

Can I identify actions that communicate high expectations for students?	
Can I describe engagement across a continuum and develop lessons to teach students about engagement?	
Can I identify reasons that students disengage and implement actions that invite them back into learning?	
Can I implement a process for developing classroom agreements and revisit these as needed?	

Access resources, tools, and guides
for this module at the companion website:
resources.corwin.com/restorativepracticesplaybook

4 RESTORATIVE CONVERSATIONS USING AFFECTIVE STATEMENTS

BELIEF STATEMENT

Power shuts down communication. Affective statements build empathic listening and reflective thinking.

A Dilemma

Bradley Ellis's classroom opens to one of the main hallways in the middle school. During passing period, he stands in his doorway to greet the students from the next class as they enter his room. He likes to make sure he has spoken to and made eye contact with each student to build relationships with them and set a positive tone for the class period.

Typically, he sees students who run through the hallway because they are late or just messing around. He consistently finds himself yelling things like "Slow down!" or "Stop running in the hallways." "You know the rules!"

Students frequently overhear him muttering to himself in exasperation about how rowdy these kids are and how they don't listen or respect the rules.

What could Mr. Ellis do or say to change the outcome of this daily occurrence?

COMMON MISCONCEPTIONS

Misconception 1: Teachers should not share their emotions or feelings with their students.

Fact: Explaining your emotions or how students' actions, words, or choices make you feel is key to helping students understand the why behind what you are asking them to do, how to behave, etc.

Misconception 2: Students know the school rules and policies so they should understand why their actions have impact.

Fact: A student may know the rules and policies but explaining why their behavior/choice/action is affecting you or other students in the context of the situation is important to help the student actually make a change.

Misconception 3: Even though students are around, they are not paying attention to teachers' conversations when talking about their day or challenges they face in the classroom or with particular students.

Fact: Students overhear and listen way more than we may realize. And even if you aren't talking about a student who is standing near you, that student internalizes what you are saying and can change their perception of you based on what they overhear.

Misconception 4: Students should understand what you mean when you say things.

Fact: Even positive words can have a negative effect on students. When you say, "Wow! *You* got that right! Good job!" or "*You* surprised me at how well you did!" what the student might actually internalize is, "My teacher didn't think I was capable of learning that or doing that. My teacher didn't expect that outcome from me. Maybe I shouldn't keep trying."

MODULE 4

SELF-ASSESSMENT

Directions: Think about the current context of your school. Use the traffic light scale to reflect on your practices as an educator. To what extent is each of these statements true?

1. I have techniques for thinking through my response to problematic behavior before I react.	
2. I use affective statements with students to promote empathetic emotions and reflective thinking.	
3. I utilize these same techniques with colleagues.	
4. I avoid punitive classroom management techniques.	

COGNITIVE REFRAMING AND RESTORATIVE CONVERSATIONS

Sometimes, it helps to view a situation from a different perspective. This is not always the case, as there are times when you have a clear view of the situation already. But sometimes, things happen that can be reframed, and your emotional state, stress level, and response might improve. It's a tool that you can use to change how the events and emotions are viewed.

There are several decades of research on cognitive reframing (Pipas & Pepper, 2021) and it has been used in a wide range of situations, from father/stepson conflicts to anxiety disorders. When the classroom or school day presents us with a situation, we naturally (and almost immediately) identify the impact of that situation on us. In other words, we frame situations as they impact us. In fact, sometimes we attribute intentionality and even malice to others because of the situation and the focus we have on ourselves. The fact is that it may have very little to do with us personally. It's just that we frame it that way and then we are hurt. It's about changing our perspectives and seeing if that improves our experience.

Cognitive reframing can help with the natural overgeneralizations that we make. As we noted earlier, our brains are pattern-detectors. But if we overgeneralize, we may miss an important lesson. For example, here are some overgeneralizations from the classroom:

- It happened once before, so it will happen again.

- That student told me that they didn't care about the last assignment, so they won't care about this one either.

- They always do that.

- That's what kids in poverty do. They will act like other students I have known.

We may not consciously be aware of these overgeneralizations, but they're just below the surface of our consciousness. We also tend to personalize. When a student is misbehaving, we tend to interpret it personally. After all, they are disrespecting the learning environment that you want to create. When we are in an argument, we all have to be aware of the tendency to attack the person rather than the evidence, especially when we have run out of evidence. Imagine the young student who has been caught doing something wrong and is eventually caught in a fib. At some point, the student is likely to say something mean or hurtful to the educator, as they have learned that adults tend to take things personally, and then the interaction changes.

WE MAY NOT CONSCIOUSLY BE AWARE OF THESE OVERGENERALIZATIONS, BUT THEY'RE JUST BELOW THE SURFACE OF OUR CONSCIOUSNESS.

We are not suggesting it is easy or that you must simply endure situations that are hurtful. We are suggesting that you can choose to reframe some of these situations while you use other techniques in this book to create long-term change in students. The benefit of cognitive reframing is that you come to realize that there are things that really have nothing to do with you. You were just there, trying to do your job. We find this to be very helpful in terms of stress and the long-term commitment educators make to their students.

We'll take you through the process of cognitive reframing with an example. You'll go through this same process with something that you have experienced that you'd like to think about differently.

Step one is to describe the situation. It helps to write things down so that you can clearly analyze the events as they occurred. Try to visualize the situation so that you can provide details.

1. Describe the event or situation.

OUR EXAMPLE	YOUR EXPERIENCE
Eleonora is on the cell phone a lot during class, even after several reminders to put it away. Eleonora is sneaky with it but is always messaging others. During class on one particular day, Eleonora was reminded six times to put the phone away, always complying without problems, but then the phone comes out again.	

The second step is to identify your feelings. When this situation arises, what is or was your emotional response? You may want to consult the color wheel (Figure 4.1) to consider the depth of the feelings you are experiencing.

Figure 4.1 Color Wheel of Emotions

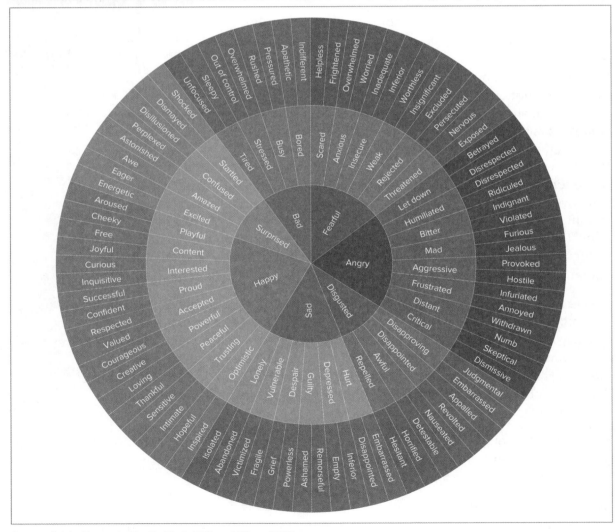

Source: Originally created by Dr. Gloria Willcox; Willcox (1982).

2. Identify your emotions and feelings.

OUR EXAMPLE	YOUR EXPERIENCE
I feel frustrated, angry, and resentful. Also, ineffective. I also experience worry that Eleonora is not learning, even though she has a perfect grade in my class.	

Once you have identified your emotions, you'll want to **examine your thoughts**. Your thoughts might arise as you identify emotions, but you'll want to spend some time with these as it will help you reframe the situation. As you explore and explain your thoughts, consider what you believe the other person's intentions were. Ask yourself what you thought would happen or what might be the impact of these events. Consider the outcomes you expected.

3. Explore and explain your thoughts.

OUR EXAMPLE	YOUR EXPERIENCE
I think that this student does not care. It's disrespectful to me and I think it makes me look bad, like I can't control the class. I expected the phone to be put away and stay away. The phone issue is taking a lot more of my time than I want to spend on it and it's making me feel like I have to be the police officer of the class. I also think it's ruining my relationship with Eleanora.	

Once your thoughts have been explored and explained, you have the opportunity to **reframe the situation or event**. Consider if the intentions of the other person or people might be different from what you thought. Might there be other reasons for the behavior or actions? Could there be other outcomes or reasons that you could consider?

4. Reframe the event or situation.

OUR EXAMPLE	YOUR EXPERIENCE
Okay, it may be that she's bored. Eleanora has a perfect score in my class, but other students see her on the phone and expect that I will do something. If not, then I could have chaos with everyone on the phone. Or it may be that she needs to communicate with someone that I don't know about— like a parent or grandparent.	

Once you have considered alternatives, you may want to test out your ideas and hypotheses. What if Eleanora needs to be in touch with a family member about something critical? Would that change how to feel about the situation? What if it is true that she's bored and has all her tasks completed? What if there is no good reason for her being on the phone so much—it's just a habit? Any of those situations could be correct and it would be interesting to know. But, before you do your investigation and perhaps even make a change, consider your emotions following the reframing and **revisit your feelings**.

5. Revisit your feelings.

OUR EXAMPLE	YOUR EXPERIENCE
I am kind of embarrassed that I am worried about what other people think. I need to have an honest conversation with Eleanora, with no one else present. But I feel a lot better thinking about this and realizing that it may not have anything to do with me. And it makes me think that it's actually a really small thing and that I'm not living up to one of the things that I say to students all the time: keep the small things small.	

AFFECTIVE STATEMENTS AND RESTORATIVE CONVERSATIONS

Affective statements are a cornerstone of restorative practices, an alternative approach to classroom and school discipline that encourages students to form emotional bonds with adults and one another while minimizing negative interactions (Costello et al., 2009). These statements draw on affect theory, which seeks to link actions to the emotions that drive them.

Well-being and satisfaction result when emotions are positive or neutral, while anger, distress, or shame result from negative emotions (Tomkins, 1962).

The theoretical basis for affective statements is grounded in the work of Carl Rogers, who pioneered nondirective therapy. He believed that unequal power structures shut down conversation, and he sought ways to shift the power structure so that the patient could engage in reflective thinking. One of his students, Thomas Gordon, developed what he called "I messages" to equip educators with a tool to accomplish similar outcomes. Gordon (2003) incorporated these into a teacher effectiveness training program as a means for educators to interact constructively with students. Affective statements further move students forward by linking these "I" messages to needs and requests.

Affective statements are used to reduce negative emotions and restore positive and neutral emotions so that the student can reintegrate into the classroom flow. Affective statements provide a way for you to share with the student that you are frustrated not with them as a person but with the actions they have taken. This allows for the separation of the deed and the doer. Students will often respond with an apology or by saying, "I didn't mean for you to feel that way." In addition, this provides space for the student to engage in reflection and positive action, rather than expending their energy on being defensive.

Affective statements often require some cognitive reframing in advance of the conversation. An initial challenge is properly labeling one's own feelings in ways that are developmentally appropriate. Face it—as teachers, we have been receiving on-the-job training since we were five years old. We have absorbed the ways our own teachers responded when they had a dust-up with a student. These responses are deeply engrained and not easily changed just by reading about affective statements. Cognitive reframing is often the first step to using affective statements. But it is also a tool for one's own empowerment. One of the delightful, and sometimes scary, things about teaching is that we're never entirely sure what the next day will bring. On many days there is true joy, but on other days an interaction with a student will bring us up short. Taking the moment to breathe, and then reframe the situation, has the effect of changing the way an event is processed by you. As has been noted by many others, you can't change the event, but you can change the way to respond to it.

AFFECT THEORY SEEKS TO LINK ACTIONS TO THE EMOTIONS THAT DRIVE THEM.

WEAVING AFFECTIVE STATEMENTS INTO THE SCHOOL DAY

It is important to remember that the language we use both toward and around students can either build their identity and agency or destroy it. Just like adults, students inevitably internalize what someone says about them or to them and begin to believe it. Using affective statements can help students understand the why behind the message you are communicating. The original frame for Gordon's (2003) "I" messages was mostly to formulate a statement that focused on how the teacher was perceiving the conflict:

1. **Give a short description of the problem behavior without assigning blame.** ("I saw that you were distracted by your phone when I was teaching that last problem.")

2. **Share the feelings you experienced because of the problem behavior.** ("I felt disappointed in myself because I want to make sure each of my students is successful.")

3. **Name the tangible effects the action had on you.** ("I'm concerned that I'll have to teach it again when you get stuck trying to do it alone.")

Affective statements build on these "I" messages by adding two more steps—a statement of need and a plan or request:

4. **Name what you value and need.** ("It's important to me that we work together.")

5. **State the plan or request.** ("Can you give me your attention for this next problem so that I can make sure you're getting the information you need to be successful?")

AFFECTIVE STATEMENTS ALLOW FOR THE SEPARATION OF THE DEED AND THE DOER.

The addition of these last two steps shifts the student to a redirection and a path for success while reducing the negative emotions that might otherwise interfere with getting the student back on track. This simple change can be a step toward building a relationship because you are now talking *with* the student rather than talking *at* them. We've included other examples of affective statements in Figure 4.2.

Figure 4.2	Examples of Affective Statements	
SITUATION	**SENTENCE STARTERS**	**EXAMPLE STATEMENTS**
A student is not engaged in class. How do you redirect them using an affective statement?	• I am so sorry that . . . • I am concerned that . . . • I am feeling frustrated about/by/to see/to hear . . .	• I am so sorry that this lesson is not capturing your attention right now. Is there anything that I should know? • I am concerned that you are going to miss some important information. How will I know that you are comfortable with the information? • I am feeling frustrated to see you check out. I tried to make a really interesting lesson. I worked on it last night.
A student is horsing around with some classmates	• I am having a hard time understanding . . .	• I am having a hard time understanding what happened. I was worried about you.

SITUATION	SENTENCE STARTERS	EXAMPLE STATEMENTS
instead of coming to the reading table. How do you fix the situation using an affective statement?	• I am so pleased by/ to see/to hear . . . • I am uncomfortable when I see/ hear . . .	• I am so pleased to see that you are ready to join our group. We missed you. I am also pleased by your understanding that you missed some time with us and that you apologized to the others in our group. • I am uncomfortable when I see you playing like that because I worry that you will get hurt. I know you like to play with friends, but I like it better when that is outside because it makes me less worried.
A student will not get off their smartphone. How do you use an affective statement so that they will put it away?	• I am uneasy about . . . • I am concerned about . . . • I am so thankful that/for . . .	• I am uneasy about your time on the phone. I am worried that there is something wrong because that is not the norm for you. • I am concerned about your phone use. I see that it's increasing, and I worry that you won't remember all the information from the class. How can I help? • I am so thankful that you are finishing up with your phone. I appreciate your responding to my request to put your phone away.

Source: Smith et al. (2021).

Choose one of the scenarios in the chart and expand it. What would a conventional response be to the situation described? How might an affective statement change the direction of the conversation? How might the student perceive it?

AFFECTIVE STATEMENTS WORK WITH ADULTS, TOO

As you interact with your colleagues during staff meetings, in the hallways or workroom, or during professional learning communities, consider applying these same principles to support your communication and relationships. This same frame works just as effectively when addressing conflict with a colleague. Your language has the power to build the identity and agency of your colleagues and the rest of the staff at your school.

Pat Evans and Carole Kipling-Ross have taught together at the same school for nearly 20 years. They are professional colleagues, as both are in the English department at their large high school. But they also readily describe themselves as friends. Over the years they have attended many celebratory occasions for each other's families, and Pat was there emotionally and in material ways when Carole's partner died three years ago.

These deep personal ties are what make their current work together quite difficult. Pat is the chair of the school's accreditation committee, a large responsibility that she takes quite seriously. She is proud of the work the school has collectively done and the evidence she and her committee have gathered is mostly positive. However, the data also raise some difficult questions about equitable practices. On several occasions, Carole has challenged Pat publicly about the data and the committee's findings. Everyone knows they're friends, and Pat has gotten the feeling that people are questioning whether Carole is her friend or not.

Pat knows that she needs to clear the air and move forward. It's important to her both professionally and personally. She chooses a time after school when she knows she and Carole will have time to discuss this without being distracted. After arriving at Carole's room and exchanging pleasantries, she shares her concern.

"Carole, I've seen that you and I have disagreed in meetings about the committee's accreditation work. In those moments, I felt embarrassed because I wasn't expecting that you and I would see this issue differently. I'm concerned that my personal feelings are getting in the way of some professional decisions I have to make. It's important to me that we're able to work together, especially when we disagree. Can you let me know what you disagree with in advance of the meeting so I can be better prepared to listen and not just react with my emotions?"

Carole is taken aback by her friend's request. "I didn't know you felt that way," she says. "It's important to me that we can have open conversations about things we don't agree on. I didn't see my professional disagreements with you as something that would cause you to feel that way. That wasn't my intention."

Over the next 10 minutes, Pat and Carole discuss their points of disagreement with the draft report and recommendations. Pat notes that she is better able to listen to Carole's reasoning because she is able to separate her professional and personal loyalties. Carole also benefits from the discussion.

"I wasn't sure you would really hear me out if we were just talking privately," Carole explains. "I thought the meeting earlier was the best place to do that. I appreciate that we hammered out a way to go forward."

UNDERMINING YOUR OWN EFFORTS: CLIP CHARTS AND OTHER PUBLIC HUMILIATION TECHNIQUES

There is a well-intended approach to classroom management that uses public humiliation to control students. In this system, teachers provide feedback to learners and the status of each learner is on public display. One example is clip charts that include a scale of behavior, with students' names on clothespins or some other device, and students move the clip up or down based on their behavior. Another example is placing students' names on the board when they misbehave and then adding checks if the behavior gets worse.

These are not restorative techniques and instead can cause anger, embarrassment, and humiliation for students. When that happens, learning is compromised. If they worked, we wouldn't be writing about them. But we all know students whose clips are on "red" every day. If they were learning from this action, they would be improving. Instead, students must do the walk of shame and change the placement of their clip based on their actions, and they must do so in front of the entire class.

THE LANGUAGE WE USE BOTH TOWARD AND AROUND STUDENTS CAN EITHER BUILD THEIR IDENTITY AND AGENCY OR DESTROY IT.

Here's a situation that is all too common: Juan is off task, and he is caught by his teacher, who tells him to clip down. Frustrated, he walks to the front of the room to move his clip, but "accidentally" bumps a few peers along the way. They complain and the teacher tells him to clip down further. He says a few things under his breath on the way back to his seat, angry at the teacher and the class, and checks out of the lesson. Later that day, the teacher calls Juan's parents to let them know what has happened. What did Juan learn from this? Most likely, the lesson was not to get caught, and nothing beyond that.

The same is true when it comes to other forms of public humiliation. Making an example out of a student by announcing their referral and need to visit the vice principal is another way that teachers exert control over students and cause shame. Again, we are not suggesting that teachers simply endure problematic behaviors from students but rather that the students learn about the impact of their actions on others. This module has focused on affective statements that help students understand that their actions have consequences. Future modules will provide additional tools that you can use to address these challenges.

YOUR LANGUAGE HAS THE POWER TO BUILD THE IDENTITY AND AGENCY OF YOUR COLLEAGUES AND THE REST OF THE STAFF AT YOUR SCHOOL.

If you are required to have a clip chart, consider flipping the clips. The best thing that happens, at the top of the chart, is a call home to families. The bottom of the chart should provide students an opportunity to re-establish a relationship with the teacher. If you use other public humiliation and shame techniques, ask yourself who is learning what. And consider more private ways of interacting with students that lets them know the impact of their actions on others. Of course, this assumes that students have a positive relationship with their teachers and peers. It really does start with a foundation of respect. Without that, a student may not care that harm was done.

In addition, you may want to consider a clip chart for yourself rather than the students. Jessica Andrade has a clip chart in her fourth-grade classroom, but the labels on the chart focus on her emotional state. When she is frustrated, she labels that emotion for students and tells them why she is feeling this way. When she is annoyed, she labels that emotion for students and tells them why. The same is true when she is relaxed, happy, or excited. Ms. Andrade models her emotional regulation for her students rather than calling them out for their behaviors and then shaming them for what they have done.

A DILEMMA: TAKE TWO

Here is how using affective statements could play out in the opening dilemma: Instead of just yelling *"Stop running in the halls!"* Mr. Ellis could approach those students and say, "Hey! I feel nervous when you mess around in the hallways during passing period. This is one of the most crowded hallways in the whole school, and I'm really concerned that someone will get hurt. Please slow down." Not only does this more clearly communicate the concern Mr. Ellis has, but it also helps the students understand how their actions affect Mr. Ellis and potentially other students. Keep in mind that this approach may not immediately eradicate the behavior, but it can make a huge difference over time in the way that students understand the kind of person Mr. Ellis is, the importance of the school rules, and the overall school climate.

Read the following scenario and consider what advice you have for the teacher and the school.

CASE IN POINT

Sasha Williams has just been hired as the principal at a struggling Title I elementary school. The school is in its third year of program improvement, but little growth has been shown in state test scores for reading and math. This is Ms. Williams's first year as principal at the school, and her focus is for teachers to use small-group instruction in reading and math. She believes that using small-group instruction will help teachers provide focused instruction at students' readiness levels and accelerate their learning.

The first-grade team is struggling with this initiative. Their class size is between 24 and 29 students. Miguel Rodriguez, a veteran teacher, is especially frustrated because he has never taught using small groups and is struggling with classroom management. Out of frustration, he vents to Julia Lybrand, one of his first-grade teammates: "Ms. Williams doesn't understand what she's asking us to do. She's so unreasonable! She has no idea how crazy my class is. There's no way I can do that this year."

How should Ms. Lybrand respond?

We have created a table of general recommendations for consideration. Add your own site-specific implications and questions that this module has provoked for you.

	BROAD RECOMMENDATIONS	SITE-SPECIFIC IMPLICATIONS AND QUESTIONS
Schoolwide	Participate in professional learning about cognitive reframing and affective statements, and practice short role-playing scenarios regularly as a staff.	
Leaders	Note your own use of affective statements and cognitive reframing in your interactions with students.	
Teachers	Identify opportunities to use cognitive reframing and affective statements in your classroom interactions. Share these with your grade level or department.	
Students	Teach students about the usefulness of identifying emotions and using affective statements to resolve small conflicts with peers.	
Family and Community	Let families know about your work on cognitive reframing and affective statements through venues where you share information about the school (e.g., newsletters, website).	

REFLECTION

Let's review the success criteria from the opening of this module. Ask yourself: Can can you do these things now? Write your reflections below.

Can I apply cognitive reframing to a situation in my own professional context?	
Can I develop affective statements to respond to common classroom situations?	
Can I implement alternatives to public humiliation?	

Access resources, tools, and guides
for this module at the companion website:
resources.corwin.com/restorativepracticesplaybook

5

RESTORATIVE CONVERSATIONS USING IMPROMPTU CONVERSATIONS

BELIEF STATEMENT

Informal, impromptu conversations reduce the need for more formal conferences, as they allow feelings and thoughts to be expressed and issues to be resolved.

A Dilemma

Cassandra Jenkins is a first-grade teacher. She spent the first two months of school working diligently with her students to help them learn the expectations for success in her classroom and the procedures for various learning experiences such as literacy centers and carpet time, as well as building a collaborative and accepting classroom community of learners. The students have practiced how to sit on the rug properly as well as how to have collaborative conversations with others in that learning space to share their thinking.

On this particular day, Ms. Jenkins's students are sitting on the rug listening to an interactive read-aloud. Like on other days, Riley is fidgety and is having a hard time sitting still. He is using a pencil from his pocket to tap other students sitting near him, causing a distraction for many others in the class. While continuing to read the book, Ms. Jenkins gives him a couple of nonverbal glances to try to correct the behavior, but it's not working. The behavior is escalating, and it's getting increasingly difficult to continue with the read-aloud.

What should Ms. Jenkins do next?

COMMON MISCONCEPTIONS

Misconception 1: An impromptu conversation is best used after students demonstrate negative behaviors, actions, or choices.

Fact: An impromptu conversation is also a powerful tool to address positive behaviors, actions, or choices to acknowledge and reinforce what the student did well and provide encouragement.

Misconception 2: Impromptu conversations should only occur between administrators and students. The teacher should not be removed from instruction to engage in an impromptu conversation.

Fact: Impromptu conversations develop communication and build relationships, which is especially important for teachers and their students. Teachers *and* administrators should engage in impromptu conversations with students to help build community within their classroom as well as throughout the school.

Misconception 3: A teacher can't leave the rest of their class unattended to have an impromptu conversation with one student during instructional time.

Fact: By engaging the rest of the class in a quick collaborative discussion (e.g., turn and talk, think-pair-share) or task, a teacher can easily hold an impromptu conversation with the necessary student during instructional time.

LEARNING INTENTIONS

- We are learning about the impact of informal conversations.
- We are learning about resolving issues locally.

SUCCESS CRITERIA

- I can describe the components of an impromptu conversation.
- I can identify the benefits of Banking Time with students and develop a plan to implement this relationship-building approach.
- I can integrate impromptu conversations into my class and resolve conflict locally.

SELF-ASSESSMENT

Directions: When relatively minor but challenging situations occur, our instinct is to tell students what they need to do and how they need to do it. We may feel better, but the student may not learn much from the experience. Or we ignore the situation and hope it gets better. Again, the student misses the opportunity to learn but, in this case, the teacher remains frustrated. For this self-assessment, consider how you might change a situation from telling the student what to do to asking them questions that allow them to develop their own solutions. This allows students to be actively involved and learn from the experience. Feel free to add your own at the end of our list and talk with others about how to accomplish this.

TELLING	ASKING
Don't bang your pencil on the table. It's distracting, and I asked you twice to stop.	
Your vocabulary choices are not appropriate for this environment. You need to stop using foul language.	
Stop talking with your classmates while I am talking. If it happens again, you'll be asked to leave.	
You are not paying attention. You need to put that down and focus.	
You left your trash on the table. You need to pick up after yourself.	
I saw you pull on her hair. Go apologize.	

PRINCIPLES AND RESEARCH ON IMPROMPTU CONVERSATIONS

Impromptu conversations are relational and informal and are consistent with the restorative culture of the school. In the United Kingdom, they call them restorative chats, which has a nice ring to it and conveys their dialogic intent (Finnis, 2021). But impromptu doesn't mean without a plan or structure. There are times when the conversation with a student needs to go a bit deeper and a simple redirect alone is not going to do an adequate job. Consider these scenarios:

- A student arrives late to your class, fails to acknowledge you, and proceeds to disrupt what was happening before her arrival by loudly announcing to classmates that she was late because she was on the phone with her boyfriend and "nothing ever happens in this class anyway."

- Three students are playing "keep away" on the playground during lunch, tossing another student's backpack to one another and just out of his reach. The other three are laughing at his distress.

- A student falls asleep in your class day after day and fails to turn in work. He's not disruptive, but he's completely disengaged.

IMPROMPTU CONVERSATIONS ARE RELATIONAL AND INFORMAL AND ARE CONSISTENT WITH THE RESTORATIVE CULTURE OF THE SCHOOL.

A conventional approach would be to refer the problem to an administrator, counselor, or dean of students. But situations like this occur a dozen times a day in some schools. There isn't enough bandwidth to have meaningful conversations with these students. So, two possible things happen. One is that the teacher turns away and tries to ignore what is happening because they know that the line of students in the principal's office is already too long. The second possibility is that overtaxed administrators who have to process infractions with so many students mete out consequences with little exploration of what's happening. First, let's do a bit of cognitive reframing:

- The late student who loudly disrupted the class doesn't want her classmates to know that the real reason she was late is that the parent who was supposed to drive her to school was already intoxicated this morning. She walked to school instead.

- One of the students participating in the bullying is afraid that if he doesn't go along, he'll be a target, too.

- The student who is falling asleep in your class is working a night job to contribute income to the household. His father has COVID and has lost his job as a driver.

It's also possible that none of these are true. But how could you possibly know without a conversation? And if the focus is solely on consequences, without the possibility of restoration, these students are deprived of the learning that can happen, while the school remains unaware that further support might be warranted.

Now consider the alternative—you've got a student who is doing really well in your class. You've noted an improvement in dispositions, or perhaps they're really making strides in a subject that has proven difficult for them. You'd never farm these conversations out to an administrator—you would absolutely find the time to share encouraging words. An impromptu conversation can also be a time to build the agency of a student, strengthen the relationship you have with them, and provide direction and reinforcement of what is working well for them.

PURPOSE AND GOALS OF IMPROMPTU CONVERSATIONS

We have expanded the definition and purpose to encompass both positive conversations as well as those used to manage some conflicts between you and the student, or among a group of students. It is important to say that this is not a one-size-fits-all approach. Restorative practices as a whole occur on a continuum, with an array of processes and protocols that are used to address varying degrees of issues that arise (Costello et al., 2009). For instance, there may be a disagreement between two students that needs to be resolved quickly. The discussion is bracketed by questions that are intended to help people express their feelings and come to agreements. Impromptu conversations are brief and are focused on returning students to the learning environment. Because these take place when the problem occurred, they should not be utilized when feelings are running high. A student who is clearly angry or bereft is not yet in an emotional space to engage. That said, impromptu conversations are useful for preventing a situation from escalating into a full-blown confrontation. In other words, it is preferable to adopt an approach "to keep the small things small" by addressing issues before they become a major problem (Positive Behaviour for Learning, 2014a).

Suppress the urge to lecture when a student has engaged in problematic behavior. As we have noted in previous modules, we all can tend to enact what we have seen in the past. We have witnessed (or been a part of) a lecture out in the school hallway, complete with a shaking finger and an admonishment to stop doing whatever had happened. These interactions are not consistent with the tenets of restorative practices, which is that adults model the use of responses that are "respectful, curious (appreciative enquiry), calm, deliberate, firm, and fair" (Thorsborne & Blood, 2013, p. 40).

It is important to note that a single conversation may not result in a sustained positive change in a student's dispositions or behavior. In practice, it is often a series of restorative conversations that is necessary for lasting change. Your continued investment in the student and your relationship with them signal that you are not giving up on them, even when they might be giving up on themselves.

PREPARING FOR AN IMPROMPTU CONVERSATION

Preparation for the impromptu conversation is brief but important. Ask yourself these questions:

- Am I ready to talk? Do I know what I will ask them?

- Are they ready to talk?

- Where is the appropriate place to have the talk? (Positive Behaviour for Learning, 2014a, p. 7)

SCRIPTING AN IMPROMPTU CONVERSATION

A script is a conversation guide. It doesn't need to be rigidly adhered to, as a chief element of an impromptu conversation is the active listening you are doing. However, a script of questions can prevent adults from wandering back into a lecture, causing the student to shut down. It is also useful to refrain from asking a student why they did something. Often, the response is going to be, "I don't know." This can also, unfortunately, lead the adult to fill in the blank for them. Some questions that can guide an impromptu conversation include

- **Tell the story:** "What happened? I'd like to hear your story first."

- **Explore the harm:** "Who do you think has been affected?"

- **Repair the harm:** "What needs to happen so that it can be right again?"

- **Reach an agreement:** What help do you need to do so?"

- **Plan a follow-up:** "What's a good time to check in with you to see how you're doing?" (adapted from Thorsborne & Vinegrad, 2004)

YOUR CONTINUED INVESTMENT IN THE STUDENT AND YOUR RELATIONSHIP WITH THEM SIGNAL THAT YOU ARE NOT GIVING UP ON THEM, EVEN WHEN THEY MIGHT BE GIVING UP ON THEMSELVES.

WHEN IT FLIES AND WHEN IT DIVES

This individual reflection is used by the New Zealand Ministry of Education's Positive Behaviour for Learning training. Think of a time when you had a conversation with a student about their behavior and it went well. Briefly describe the incident and conversation and note the factors that contributed to the conversation being so effective. How do you know it went well? Then do the same for a conversation that didn't go well and was ineffective.

When It Flies

Incident:

Conversation:

Factors that made the conversation effective:

When It Dives

Incident:

Conversation:

Factors that made the conversation ineffective:

BANKING TIME

As we have noted, restorative practices work best when there is a strong relationship between the teacher and student and students with their peers. One way to build and maintain relationships with students, especially those who are hard to reach, is Banking Time. Developed by Pianta and colleagues (e.g., Driscoll & Pianta, 2010), the idea is much like a savings account. The teacher and student interact, making deposits into their shared account. When something not so good happens, there is a reserve. If there is nothing in the metaphorical savings account and something unpleasant occurs, the relationship is likely to be damaged and feelings get hurt. Banking Time sessions are not dependent on students' behavior, meaning that we don't engage in Banking Time as a reward for positive behaviors or when a student displays a problematic behavior. These sessions occur on a regular basis with the students who need them. Of course, not all your students will need Banking Time sessions.

As Alamos et al. (2018) note, Banking Time is a "dyadic, short-term intervention to improve the quality of teacher–child interactions between a teacher and a specific child, building a more positive teacher–child relationship" (p. 437). During these brief (10- to 15-minute) interactions, the teacher and student interact in an activity chosen by the learner. The student leads the interaction, and the teacher can narrate but avoids directing the interaction, asking questions, or giving praise. Alamos et al. (2018) noted that there were really three profiles of teachers when it came to the actual implementation of Banking Time:

1. **High fidelity,** in which the teachers engaged in the child's activity while ensuring that the child led the session

2. **Low engaged,** in which the child led the session, but the teacher was not engaged in the child's activity

3. **Teacher-led,** in which the teacher was engaged in the child's activity but also directing the session instead of ensuring the child's lead (p. 437)

The relationships that developed as a result of these three different profiles were noteworthy, with the strongest bonds occurring in the first condition and the weakest in the third.

Pilar is often disruptive, impulsive, and loud. Her teacher decides to implement Banking Time to get to know Pilar better. They spend about 10 minutes together three times per week. During these sessions, Pilar directs the activity. Sometimes she wants to draw. Other times Pilar wants to read a book, and still other times she engages in imaginative play. Her teacher, Jeffrey Watkins, begins by observing. As they interact, Mr. Watkins labels actions and emotions: "You're smiling at that part of the book. You must really like what the character said."

Mr. Watkins also narrates actions, as was the case when Pilar was drawing. At one point, Mr. Watkin says, "You're erasing some lines. And I see that you're revising as you go." When Pilar becomes frustrated with the drawing, Mr. Watkins uses a calm voice and says, "I'm here to help when you want. Is there something that is frustrating you? You can trust me."

Pilar responds that it doesn't look right, pointing to a face that she has drawn.

Mr. Watkins responds, "You're the artist and I'm here to help when I can. We have lots of paper and we have time. Would you like to practice on a different paper and see what you think?" They continue their interaction with Pilar sketching on a scrap piece of paper.

YOUR ROLE IS TO GIVE THE STUDENT (OR SOMETIMES A SMALL GROUP OF STUDENTS) YOUR UNDIVIDED ATTENTION AND TO SHOW INTEREST IN THEIR CHOICES.

There are several noteworthy actions that Mr. Watkins took. Note that he did not praise or ask a lot of questions. Mr. Watkins also did not take over or use commands. He sent a clear message that he was not leaving when Pilar became frustrated and that there were ways to deal with the frustrations that occurred. In general, Banking Time sessions include the following:

- **Following the student's lead.** Limit the teacher-type questions, directions, and commands. Rather, allow the student to direct the activity and use the materials as they choose, provided that they are safe.

- **Observing.** Make mental notes about the student's behavior, feelings, language, and actions. Also, take note of your reactions to the interaction.

- **Narrating.** Use language to describe what the student is doing. There are a number of ways to do this, according to the Center for Advanced Study of Teaching and Learning (n.d.), including the *sportscaster,* in which you describe play by play, using *reflection* in which you comment on the students' language and share back, and *imitation,* in which you mimic what the student is doing.

- **Labeling emotions.** Verbally comment on the positive and negative emotions that are expressed by the student. These expressions from the student might be verbal or nonverbal. Your role is to notice and comment.

- **Developing relational themes.** These comments send a message to the student that they are important and that you value the relationship.

Remember, Banking Time is not instructional time. Your role is to give the student (or sometimes a small group of students) your undivided attention and to show interest in their choices. You can use language as we have noted above, but refrain from trying to teach a skill or direct the learning.

Some educators tell us that they do not have time for banking with students. And yes, academic instruction is critical, and students deserve to learn. But the question we ask when time issues are raised is this: Are all your students benefiting from the academic lessons you provide? If not, could a 10-minute investment, several times per week, increase the relational trust in the classroom and increase the impact that your academic lessons have? Or, to consider another question: Are there students whose problematic behavior is interfering with their learning? If so, why not try Banking Time and see if the development of a stronger relationship improves your job satisfaction and students' learning?

QUESTIONS TO CONSIDER	POSSIBILITIES YOU IDENTIFY	QUESTIONS I HAVE
Who is one student who might benefit from 10-minute conversations, about three times a week, with me?		
Where might I find time to do this?	• During recess • During lunch time • During independent work • During collaborative work	
How will I know it is successful?		
Who at my site or district might be able to support me in learning more about Banking Time?		

2 × 10 TECHNIQUE

There is another process that teachers can use to develop strong relationships with students: the 2 × 10 approach (Ginsberg & Wlodkowski, 2004). The 2 × 10 strategy generally works well to get a relationship started. The idea is to spend 2 minutes per day, for 10 consecutive days, interacting with a student. The key to this is that the interaction is about anything other than school. Topics can include hopes and dreams, fears, likes and dislikes, family life, work situations, or just about anything that allows a relationship to develop. For some adults, it's hard to remember that a relationship is reciprocal, meaning that the adult needs to share about their life as well as invite the student to share.

YOU ARE THE ADULT. DON'T HAVE HURT FEELINGS. BE PERSISTENT AND DON'T GIVE UP.

Jessica Shawley, in the PE Blog (n.d.), outlined some thinking that is useful when considering the implementation of the 2 × 10 strategy. Note the references to physical education, but you can make them your own.

- **Who?** Though you cannot reach all students right away, you have to start somewhere. Pick one or two students per class to focus on. This doesn't mean you neglect the others; it just means you will be intentional with these because the relationship needs building, they need extra support because of something going on at home, or they have been a discipline issue and you do not want them to get out of control.

- **When will you speak with them?** Before class? At the end of class? During warm-ups (all the more reason for self-directed instant warm-ups)? During circuit training stations or transitions? Can they help with equipment? Create opportunities for connection. You may even just have to be their partner for an activity. Anthony's tennis partner was gone a few days. I learned so much about this kid just by asking questions as we worked through tennis drills. I don't have any problems with him anymore and I now know how rough home is for him. He's doing well, all considered.

- **What will you talk about?** Ask open-ended questions. What are your interests outside of school? What did you think about today's lesson? How did you like the activity?

- **What if they don't seem like they want to talk to you?** Then you do the talking! You are the adult. Don't have hurt feelings. Be persistent and don't give up. By the tenth day, they will be the one doing all the talking. Believe me, Josh has a hard time being quiet while he helps me take down and pack up the pedometer station each day. I've learned more about teenage boy fashion preferences than I thought I ever could.

- **Smile and be a persistent, positive role model.** Inevitably, this strategy will work with any student though I chose to highlight the 2 × 10 theory in the context of challenging students because I think it is a helpful analogy to remember: Use that 2 × 10 piece of lumber to help build a bridge and connect with the student rather than make them walk the plank! (Shawley, n.d.)

Sometimes teachers start with an open-ended question such as "*Who* do you want to be and *what* do you want to be?" Or you might take turns filling in the blank: "If you knew me, you would know . . ." The point is to get to know the student and for the student to know you. As we like to say, "It's harder to be disrespectful to someone when you know their story." Once a relationship has been established, the conversations can move to include academic and behavioral concerns. That doesn't mean that no further relationship development is necessary but rather that the interactions can now include discussions about expectations, feedback about performance, and plans for correction. The key elements that are essential for impromptu conversations like 2 × 10 and those that we discuss in the next section are:

- **Brevity.** These conversations typically last under 2 minutes.

- **Voice.** Students are invited to share their versions of the events.

- **Honesty.** Teachers share their own feelings.

- **Accountability.** Students aren't threatened with punishment, but they are reminded that they are accountable to others.

- **Solution-oriented.** Students are invited to suggest ways to resolve the problem.

QUESTIONS TO CONSIDER	POSSIBILITIES YOU IDENTIFY	QUESTIONS I HAVE
Who is one student who might benefit from a 2 × 10 set of conversations?		
Where might I find time to do this?	• During recess • During passing periods • During lunch time • During independent work • During collaborative work	

(Continued)

(Continued)

QUESTIONS TO CONSIDER	POSSIBILITIES YOU IDENTIFY	QUESTIONS I HAVE
How will I know it is successful?		
Who at my site or district might be able to support me in learning more about 2 × 10?		

WEAVING IMPROMPTU CONVERSATIONS INTO THE SCHOOL DAY

The goal of impromptu conversations is to build communication and relationships between you and your students, so the classroom environment plays an important role in their success. Focus on building a collaborative classroom environment where students frequently discuss their questions and thoughts or engage in interactive activities at different points throughout instruction. This opens the opportunity to have impromptu conversations with students during those collaborative moments, if needed, without taking away instructional time from the rest of the class.

Another way to build opportunities for impromptu conversations is through the physical spaces in your classroom. Having a cool-down corner or an emoji check-in board provides students with an easy way to communicate that they need time to speak with you. Providing students with journals (for writing and/or drawing) is another method of communication that you can use to gauge whether impromptu conversations are needed.

Keep in mind that impromptu conversations should not be limited to in-class situations. You can also look for signs that an impromptu conversation is needed during transition times throughout the school day/outside of the classroom. For example, do you notice that a student is rubbing their eyes when you pick them up from recess? Do you see a student walking slouched with their head down while they throw away their trash in the cafeteria? Is a student walking extremely slowly on purpose to and from the restroom? Does a student always try to get in trouble right before heading to a certain class period or at the end of the day on Fridays? All these signs present an opportunity to engage in an impromptu conversation.

There are multiple times during the day that you can have an impromptu conversation with a student. For example, while students are working collaboratively or independently, you can engage several students in a row in these brief interactions. You can also plan times during your day for this should the need arrive on a given day. That may be during a transition, when students know the expectation of putting things away and getting ready for the next task, or a time when students are engaged in reflections and writing. When educators see the value of these conversations and the impact that they have, they find the time to engage in these conversations with their students.

STEALING THE CONFLICT

Throughout this module and the previous one that focused on affective statements, we have described the restorative conversations that educators have with students. In each of these cases, the seriousness of harm was low, and it was important for educators to allow students to see how their actions and behavior caused harm. They also focused on what could occur next as students made amends and commitments for the future.

The point we want to make here is that the educator and the student were able to interact and resolve the conflict. There are times in which the actions are serious and will require more intervention, as will be the case when we discuss restorative conferences. For example, it is quite possible that the bullying incident we discussed earlier requires more intervention, and an impromptu conversation will be inadequate. But a more common occurrence in some schools is to have someone else, such as an administrator or dean of students, talk with the student when there is a problem. Again, this is appropriate when the harm is serious. But it's less appropriate when the harm is low level and the educator (or peers) needs to be able to express their feelings and thoughts.

WHEN EDUCATORS SEE THE VALUE OF THESE CONVERSATIONS AND THE IMPACT THAT THEY HAVE, THEY FIND THE TIME TO ENGAGE IN THESE CONVERSATIONS WITH THEIR STUDENTS.

When someone else intervenes on your behalf in a low-stakes situation, the conflict is stolen away from the person who experienced the harm. Let's consider an example. Martin refuses to open his book. He says, "This class is boring" and he provokes other students to join his protest. The teacher, justifiably frustrated, sends him to the principal's office. Martin strolls in the hallway, stopping along the way a few times before arriving in the front office.

He is greeted by the person working the front desk and asked to take a seat. A few minutes later, the principal asks Martin to come into the office. Once inside, the principal asks Martin what happened. Martin confesses to saying that the class was boring and yelling to his peers. When asked why, Martin responds that he doesn't know. The principal admonishes him and asks for a commitment that he will treat the teacher with respect. The entire exchange lasts about 4 minutes. But the principal knows that Martin cannot yet return to class as the teacher expects there to be some consequences, so Martin is asked to get on his laptop and complete one of his reading activities. Twenty minutes later, Martin is asked to return to the classroom.

As he enters, a few peers say "Ohhhhh," and the teacher asks them to quiet down and then returns to the lesson. Inside, however, the teacher is still upset and does not have a sense of closure and resolve. It's very likely that this teacher will be watching Martin more closely for additional actions that would justify sending him to the principal again.

Let's flip this script. Instead of sending Martin to the principal, what if the teacher asked the principal to supervise the class while the students engaged in their collaborative tasks? And then the teacher had a private conversation with Martin about his actions and behaviors? The teacher could use affective statements to start an impromptu conversation to avoid shame and blame, make the point that feelings were hurt, and send the message that this is not the Martin that the teacher knows. When asked by his teacher, Martin explains that the text was too hard, that the person sitting next to him teased him for being stupid, and that he was hungry.

The teacher apologizes that someone said Martin was stupid, adding, "I see you as a dedicated student who works very hard. Last week, you told me you were proud of your accomplishments in our class. What can I do to help you feel comfortable with this text? You know, it's hard for everyone. We are going to read and talk about it for a few days to figure out what it means. The Martin I know likes a challenge."

Martin apologizes, saying he was rude because his feelings were hurt and that he did not mean to hurt the teacher. "You're always so nice to me. I'm sorry that I did that. I hope you still like me."

Assured that he was still valued, the teacher says, "So, tell me about being hungry. What's going on?" Martin explains that the new baby was getting all the attention and that he had to make breakfast himself, but that day he was late and didn't eat. The teacher says, "We can solve this" and sends him to the cafeteria with a note.

When Martin returns a few minutes later, he feels great and engaged in the learning task. But equally importantly, his teacher feels great having learned something about Martin and being able to express her feelings about the situation. She resolves to check in with him each morning to make sure that his day was off to a good start and to announce to the class when she expected students to grapple with ideas in the texts she selected.

A DILEMMA: TAKE TWO

Ms. Jenkins' redirections haven't worked with Riley, and she has noticed this pattern before. She decides to give Riley a different task to do so that she can finish the interactive read-aloud.

"Riley, I'm realizing that I could really use your help right now. Could you come up here and sit by me to help me hold the book?" The student gets up from the rug and positions herself next to the teacher. After Ms. Jenkins finishes the read-aloud, she makes an adjustment to her lesson plan so that she can get some time to hold an impromptu conversation with Riley.

"Here's our next task, everyone. Please meet with your table group to make a collaborative poster of a part of the story," says Ms. Jenkins. "Draw your favorite scene in one corner of the chart, write a description, and be sure to write your name. Then you can take turns telling one another about the part you selected and why." She pulls out chart paper and markers for each table and reviews the directions for this familiar activity.

"Riley, let's meet over at our conversation corner," says Ms. Jenkins, motioning to two comfortable chairs and a table she has in the room. After they get situated, Ms. Jenkins begins.

TELL THE STORY

"I could see that you were distracted during the read-aloud," she says. "I'd like to hear your story. What was happening?"

The student replies that she just wanted to tell Amanda something, but Amanda wouldn't turn around. "So I tapped her with my pencil so she would pay attention to me."

EXPLORE THE HARM

"Hmm, that can be hard when you really want to tell someone something right now and they won't listen," said Ms. Jenkins. "Could it be that Amanda was paying attention to the story?" Riley concedes that this is probably true, so Ms. Jenkins continues. "I notice that you get wiggly during rug time on other days. I want to be sure that you get all the learning time you deserve. How does this hurt your learning?"

Riley replies, "Well, I don't know the story."

Ms. Jenkins nods. "You're right. And when you don't know the story, who else gets hurt?" Riley thinks for a minute, and then says, "I can't help my group so good."

Ms. Jenkins is pleased to see that Riley has some self-awareness and decides that she doesn't need to discuss how it impacted her as a teacher.

REPAIR THE HARM

Moving forward, she asks, "What needs to happen so that it can be right the next time we're working at the rug?"

Riley hesitates, then says, "I need to sit at the side of the rug, so I'm not distracted."

Ms. Jenkins is surprised at this; it wasn't a solution she had considered.

REACH AN AGREEMENT

"So, let's try that for a week," says the teacher. "What help are you going to need to do so?"

Riley says, "Can you remind me to sit on the side of the rug? I might forget and sit with Amanda."

Ms. Jenkins smiles. "Yes, of course I can do that."

PLAN A FOLLOW-UP

"Let's check in with each other again next Tuesday to see how it's working for you and for me," Ms. Jenkins says. The teacher then turns her attention back to the class. "I can't wait to see what all of you are doing! I'm coming around to visit all the tables."

Read the following scenario and consider what advice you have for the teacher and the school.

 CASE IN POINT

Henry Tsu teaches eighth-grade pre-algebra. He loves teaching mathematics and does his best to make class fun for students. As a result of the COVID-19 pandemic, he and the other pre-algebra teachers on campus have begun using more videos to support their instruction. This is really helping his students make mathematical connections and build their academic language, and he feels they are more engaged in class as well.

Recently, a new student named Rashad transferred into Mr. Tsu's class from another school. Rashad is struggling with the content in class and does not participate often. Mr. Tsu has tried to help by allowing the student more time to complete assignments, but it doesn't seem to help.

One day, Rashad is trying his best to keep up with the video and note-taking assignment when he becomes visibly frustrated. He throws down his pencil on the desk, shoves himself in his seat back from his desk, and yells, "F*** this class! I hate it!"

Immediately, the class turns to look at Rashad. Mr. Tsu, shocked by the behavior and blatant disrespect, sends Rashad out into the hallway and resumes working with the rest of the class.

What advice do you have for Mr. Tsu? What support might teachers at this school need?

RECOMMENDATIONS AND IMPLICATIONS

We have created a table of general recommendations for consideration. Add your own site-specific implications and questions that this module has provoked for you.

	BROAD RECOMMENDATIONS	SITE-SPECIFIC IMPLICATIONS AND QUESTIONS
Schoolwide	Read and practice to learn about impromptu conversations. Identify as a school where they might best be utilized.	
Leaders	Develop procedures to help avoid stealing the conflict. Support teachers to host their own impromptu conversations with your assistance.	
Teachers	Identify times when you can host Banking Time, 2 × 10, and impromptu conversations during your day.	
Students	Teach students proactively about the scripts for impromptu conversations (Tell the Story, Explore the Harm, etc.) to build their capacity to participate in them.	
Family and Community	Share Banking Time procedures with families so that they can also host conversations at home.	

REFLECTION

Let's review the success criteria from the opening of this module. Ask yourself: Can you do these things now? Write your reflections below.

Can I describe the components of an impromptu conversation?	
Can I identify the benefits of Banking Time with students and develop a plan to implement this relationship-building approach?	
Can I integrate impromptu conversations into my class and resolve conflict locally?	

Access resources, tools, and guides
for this module at the companion website:
resources.corwin.com/restorativepracticesplaybook

6

RESTORATIVE CIRCLES

BELIEF STATEMENT

Restorative circles allow participants to engage in conflict resolution, healing, and decision making through honest conversations and relationship building.

A Dilemma

It's December, and Ms. Garcia's kindergarten class has been working hard all year to live by their class agreements:

In our class…

We work hard and do our best.

We use kind words and help each other.

We are loved and valued for who we are.

We are Walker Elementary Wolverines!

Over the past few weeks, Ms. Garcia has noticed that students are tattling on each other more frequently. She has done her best to address each instance directly and tied students' behavior and attitudes back to their class agreements to promote the important values and beliefs that they are working toward this year. However, it doesn't seem to be shifting the trend of more discord. Ms. Garcia is growing more frustrated, especially because the tattling is often taking away from learning opportunities throughout the day.

One day, as Ms. Garcia goes to pick her class up from recess, she is swarmed with students talking over each other, each tattling something different about what happened during recess. Immediately overwhelmed, Ms. Garcia says, "Okay, friends, everyone needs to stop talking. I can't hear anything anyone is saying," but the students have so much to share they just can't stop. She motions with her hands up to help them calm down and thinks about what she should do next.

What should Ms. Garcia do next?

COMMON MISCONCEPTIONS

Misconception 1: Restorative circles should only be used to address punitive issues.

Fact: While restorative circles can definitely be used to address classroom challenges such as a negative report from a substitute or an instance where the class as a whole is not meeting class/school expectations, they are also an effective way to foster community by discussing positive events and academic content.

Misconception 2: Restorative circles take away too much valuable instructional time.

Fact: Circles can be used to build a sense of belonging and community of learners when applied to academic content (e.g., "After conducting an experiment, what surprised you most?" or "After reading a piece of informational text, what is one word you feel is important to understanding the concept?").

Misconception 3: Restorative circles are the best way to address any misbehavior issue.

Fact: If there is a specific incident that has occurred between a few students (e.g., there is someone who has done harm and someone who has been harmed), it is likely more appropriate to specifically address the incident using a restorative conference between just the affected students.

Misconception 4: "My classroom isn't big enough for everyone to get into an actual circle shape, so I shouldn't use circles."

Fact: The goal is to have everyone in a circle so that all students are seen when they are sharing, are included in discussion, and don't feel hidden. If your classroom isn't big enough for a complete circle, do the best you can or consider using another space in the school that is conducive to the discussion you intend to have during the circle.

LEARNING INTENTIONS

- I am learning about restorative circles and their use.

SUCCESS CRITERIA

- I can identify three components that are consistently used in all circles.

- I can describe and apply the phases of a restorative circle.

- I can compare and contrast various types of circles and decide when to use each.

SELF-ASSESSMENT

CONDITION	IN PLACE	PARTIALLY IN PLACE	NOT IN PLACE
Circles are used both in classroom and nonclassroom settings.			
Circles are used for community building/welcoming.			
Circles are used for restoring or repairing harm.			
Purpose of circle is clearly stated before the circle begins.			
Restorative circles, or other circles to repair harm, are co-facilitated by a trained staff person, administrator, or other person as agreed upon by staff.			
Students have contributed to establishment of circle values.			
Circle keeper is identified for each circle event (can be staff or student).			
Circle keeper consistently states circle guidelines.			
Circle keeper initiates dialogue using a talking piece.			
Circle keeper provides the opportunity for all participants to speak in turn.			

Source: Illinois Balanced and Restorative Justice (n.d.).

PRINCIPLES OF RESTORATIVE CIRCLES

More than any other dimension of restorative practices, restorative circles directly reflect their roots in indigenous cultures across the world. The circle is understood as a form of community dialogue where members can allow for all voices to be heard in an environment that is neutral. Rather than relying on a single leader, the community enacts principles of direct democracy, providing the community with a platform to reach consensus, make decisions, and self-govern.

Before we discuss the format and procedures of restorative circles, let's focus first on their major purposes, as the purpose is what drives the format selected. The purposes for a restorative circle include

- Contributing to a positive classroom and school culture that values voice and choice and ensures learning

- Assisting students in working through issues and situations that impact their classroom academically and socially, whether directly or indirectly

- Building the capacity of classroom and school communities to arrive at consensus, make decisions, and take action

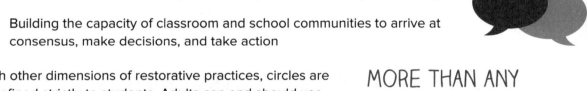

As with other dimensions of restorative practices, circles are not confined strictly to students. Adults can and should use restorative circles in professional learning communities and grade or department meetings, when appropriate, to work through an issue that is challenging the group. At the school where we work, the circle is how we begin each day. The entire certificated and classified staff (more than 70 adults) stand in a circle to discuss three items:

- What do we need to know for today?

- What students need a spotlight for praise or concern?

- A culture-building prompt that allows one staff member each day to publicly reflect

MORE THAN ANY OTHER DIMENSION OF RESTORATIVE PRACTICES, RESTORATIVE CIRCLES DIRECTLY REFLECT THEIR ROOTS IN INDIGENOUS CULTURES ACROSS THE WORLD.

Our morning meeting lasts only 10 minutes but because it is daily, it provides a way for the organization to continually invest in its relational culture. Adults know that they will see each other every morning, allowing them to engage in short conversations after the meeting. It has also become a forum for further problem solving. Teachers will routinely spotlight a student for concern, followed by a request to meet briefly after the meeting with others who have a relationship with that student. Our point is not to argue that your school should enact a morning circle meeting but rather that the versatile nature of circles makes it a tool for use across the school.

Whether used by students or adults, a restorative circle has its own set of agreements that each member should abide by. It is useful to review these at the start of any restorative circle. These circle principles include the following, which we encourage you to co-construct with your own students so that they own the language. These are suggestions adapted from Positive Behaviour for Learning (2014b):

- Confidentiality is maintained.

- Respectful language is used.

- The only person who talks is the one with the talking piece.

- We listen with respect.

- We speak from the heart.

- We focus on solutions.

- We seek a positive outcome.

Directions: Revisit Module 3's section on classroom agreements. What are the similarities between restorative circle agreements and classroom agreements? What are unique characteristics? We have started a list in the Venn diagram in Figure 6.1. Continue to fill in characteristics.

Figure 6.1   Restorative Circle Agreements and Classroom Agreements

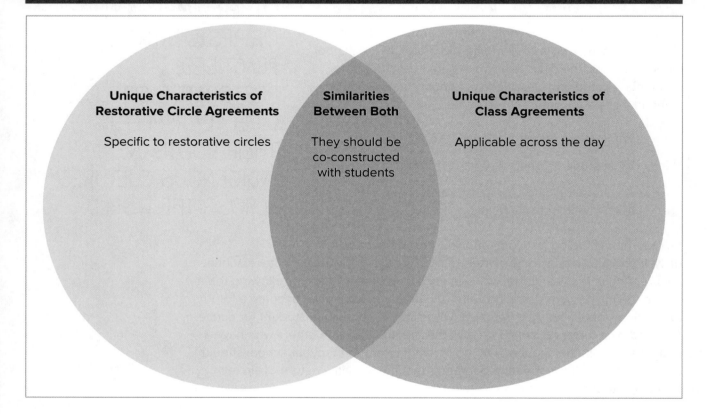

Unique Characteristics of Restorative Circle Agreements

Specific to restorative circles

Similarities Between Both

They should be co-constructed with students

Unique Characteristics of Class Agreements

Applicable across the day

COMPONENTS OF EVERY CIRCLE

Regardless of the type of circle needed, there are three components that are a consistent factor in the way that circles operate. These are important considerations, and if they are not available, the circle should be delayed. They really are that important and each is critical to the success of the circle. If one or more is missing, the circle is not likely to be successful and participants may come to believe that circles are ineffective.

1. **Meeting space.** It's called a circle for a reason. That structure allows each person to see every other person. A circle has no starting place or ending place, and there is no position of power. Of course, there are formal and informal power dynamics in every classroom, but the circle visually signifies that each member is important and valued. Ideally, there are no desks or other items that block the circle. We are all more vulnerable and open with one another when our bodies are not blocked by furniture. Sometimes, this is not possible in the classroom, but ideally, the circle is just chairs. In some cases, there is a symbolic object in the center of the circle that reminds participants about the purpose of the circle, their agreements, or the commitments they have made to one another.

2. **Talking piece.** Using an object to indicate who is speaking at a given time helps to ensure respect for the speaker and the listeners. It helps remind members of the circle not to interrupt the speaker, even though this is hard for all of us to do. The talking piece is passed from person to person, and only the person holding the talking piece can speak. Ideally, the talking piece is symbolic and meaningful for the group. Since a goal of circles and class meetings is to build community, making the talking piece something significant to you/your class is one way to make the experience personal. For example, the talking piece could be a mini soccer ball if you and your class love soccer, or a paintbrush if you all like art/drawing. If the group has had a shared experience, such as a field trip, the talking piece could be a reminder of that event. It may also be a mascot or object that represents a shared value. And the talking piece can change over time or be based on the purpose of the circle or as you and your class grow together or change interests.

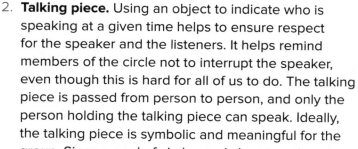

IF THESE THREE COMPONENTS ARE NOT AVAILABLE, THE CIRCLE SHOULD BE DELAYED.

3. **Circle keeper.** The keeper starts the conversations and guides the conversation. But the circle keeper does not interject as others are speaking, other than to maintain the agreements of the circle. The circle keeper can be an adult or student. But the circle keeper needs to understand their role and recognize that they are also a member of the circle, even as they monitor the process. If the circle has been organized

to address harm, the circle keeper cannot be one of those harmed. If the harm is widespread within a classroom, the circle keeper may need to be someone outside of the class, such as another teacher, counselor, or school leader. Ideally, the circle keeper is supportive, nonjudgmental, a good listener, respectful, and approachable. In the best-case scenario, there are training opportunities for circle keepers, and those sessions are provided to students in age-appropriate ways.

Have you been a part of a restorative circle? Were these guidelines followed? If so, how did they contribute to the process? If not, how would their presence have improved the process you participated in?

THE PHASES OF A CIRCLE MEETING

As we have noted, there are any number of reasons that a circle may be scheduled. But we must say this again: circles are not limited to addressing problematic behavior. Regardless of the type of circle, there are generally phases that the group will go through. Some of the phases will be shortened as the group becomes accustomed to circles.

PHASE 1: GROUNDING

The first phase is introductory. Some people call this grounding or focusing. The idea for this first phase is to welcome members to the circle, establish the group expectations, and generally check in with the members of the group. Depending on the purpose of the circle, this may be brief or more extended. If the talking piece is new, it is introduced at this time. The circle keeper may ask participants what they hope to gain from this circle or may establish the purpose of the conversation. There may be time devoted during this introductory phase to deepen relationships between the participants. There are a number of ways to strengthen relationships, and the amount of time devoted to this phase will depend on how well the group knows each other as well on as the goal of the circle.

PHASE 2: THE STORY AND ITS IMPACT

The next phase focuses on the story and the impact of the topic. The conversation deepens here to focus on the purpose of the circle and the experiences people have had with the topic being discussed. This may include participants talking about their needs and interests or may focus on memories and experiences. The goal is to ensure that participants have the opportunity to express the ways in which they are thinking about the event, situation, or topic. If there has been harm done, participants express that. If there are celebrations, people share that.

PHASE 3: HEALING OR OPTIONS

The group then focuses on healing or options. They may discuss strengths that they, or the group, have. Or they may discuss repairs that need to occur. The goal is to focus on what will make things right, to create positive change, or to acknowledge success. As the group explores options, they will likely become unstuck and begin to see that there are actions they can individually and collectively take to address the topic at hand.

PHASE 4: CONSENSUS BUILDING

The final phase is consensus building and reaching agreement. If the circle has focused on an action that individuals need to take, the goal is for participants to be able to live with the outcome. Reaching agreements takes time and increases the likelihood that members of the circle will own and support the decision, personally committing to the next steps. One way for the circle keeper to check in with members of the group is to use a consensus level system. For example:

REACHING AGREEMENTS TAKES TIME AND INCREASES THE LIKELIHOOD THAT MEMBERS OF THE CIRCLE WILL OWN AND SUPPORT THE DECISION, PERSONALLY COMMITTING TO THE NEXT STEPS.

1: I totally agree with the decision or action. I fully support this.

2: I find the decision or action acceptable and will support it.

3: I can live with the decision or action, but I am not fully supportive.

4: I do not fully agree with the decision or action, but I will not block it. I trust the group, but I want others to understand why I am reserved.

5: I do not agree with the decision or action, and I will probably attempt to block it or not take action.

6: I do not think we have an agreement, and we need more time to work.

When each participant selects a level between 1 and 4, consensus is reached. The concerns raised by individuals who select 3 or 4 should be addressed by the group, but action and implementation are likely. If any member chooses a 5 or 6, consensus is not reached at that time. The group needs more discussion, which may need to be delayed, but know that action and implementation will be limited.

PLAN YOUR CIRCLE

Use the following planning guide to ensure that all the components necessary for an effective circle are present.

ASPECT	CONSIDERATIONS	NOTES
Setting	• Is it a true physical circle? • Can participants see each other?	
Talking piece	• Is the item familiar? • Does a new talking piece need to be introduced?	
Circle keeper	• Who will guide the process? • Who might be a backup if needed?	
Norms and agreements	• Are the norms and agreements familiar? • Do new norms or agreements need to be developed? • How will they be shared or revisited?	
Introduction	• How will participants be welcomed? • How will the purpose of the circle be established? • Is there a need for relationship building?	
Deepening and exploring impact	• Which questions will be asked to encourage participants to share stories? • What questions will allow participants to describe their impact? • Who has been affected and in what ways?	
Repairs or actions	• How will ideas for resolution or action be shared? • How will the conversation center on healing or positive change?	
Consensus	• How will you know that consensus has been reached? • What actions may need to be taken if consensus is not reached?	

TYPES OF RESTORATIVE CIRCLES

As you consider using circles and class meetings in your classroom, here are some different strategies for implementation:

- **Sequential circles.** The entire class creates one large circle in the room. After the prompt or discussion question is shared, one student is given a talking piece. That student shares what they would like to say and then passes the talking piece to the person next to them until all students around the circle have shared. A student may pass the talking piece without sharing, but typically all students respond.

- **Nonsequential circles.** The entire class creates one large circle in the room. After the prompt or discussion question is shared, one student begins with the talking piece and shares what they would like to say. The talking piece moves anywhere around the circle, as students volunteer to share. A wise practice is to have the speaker return the talking piece to the center of the circle when they are done speaking. The next person to speak retrieves it from the center in order to continue the discussion. This saves the last speaker from awkwardly asking who wants to speak next and instead shifts the responsibility to the group as a whole.

- **Inside-outside circles.** The class is divided into two equal groups. The students make two circles, one inside the other, and the two circles face each other. After the prompt or discussion question is shared, each pair of students facing each other discusses. When discussion is finished, the outside circle stays still and the inside circle moves one person to the right, providing each student with a new discussion partner. The rotation continues as appropriate to the topic being discussed or the lesson requires.

- **Fishbowl circles.** The class creates one large circle in the room. A small group of students move to the center of the circle and enter into a discussion. Typically, the discussion is a problem-solving situation, but the focus can change depending on the needs of the class and the learning opportunity. Place an empty chair in the fishbowl so that others can join as needed. The students in the large circle act as observers of the discussion occurring in the fishbowl circle. When appropriate, the observers provide their input, observations, and ideas.

Have your students had experiences with each of these kinds of circles? Check all that apply.

CIRCLE TYPE	NO EXPERIENCE	FOR ACADEMIC LEARNING	FOR SOCIAL-EMOTIONAL LEARNING
Sequential circles			
Nonsequential circles			
Inside-outside circles			
Fishbowl circles			

Analyze your responses. Where are there opportunities to implement circles? What can you teach others?

WEAVING RESTORATIVE CIRCLES INTO THE SCHOOL DAY

Restorative circles depend on the trust students have with other members, and of the process itself. As a school, we learned early on that it was a mistake to only use restorative circles when a problem arose. It didn't take long for students to figure out that if they were asked to move their chairs into a circle formation, it was because something negative had occurred.

"Okay, who did it?" a student asked one day without even knowing what the issue was. "Let's skip the circle and get this over with." Oops.

Build restorative circles proactively by using them at the start of the day or class period to check in with your students through a low-stakes social-emotional prompt or question. Questions could pertain directly to the school day, such as "What is one goal you have for yourself this week?" or more generally, such as "What is something that you think about or do that makes you happy, even when you're feeling down?" This signals that circles are used routinely and in ways that are emotionally safe. It also gives students practice in rehearsing the circle agreements and routines.

Restorative circles provide a forum to discuss something that has occurred in the class, in the school, or in the world. For example, in the aftermath of a natural disaster, restorative class circles can be used to support students as they come back to school. In the aftermath of devastating fires in California in 2019 that destroyed communities, the California Teachers Association (CTA) developed a toolkit for educators to use in restorative circles as schools came back together. They recommended that circle keepers begin by saying,

> The fires have impacted all of us. It is normal to have many different emotions and reactions. Some of you may feel scared, angry, guilty, shocked, or relieved. These emotions may change and may last a while. I want you to know that this school is a safe place and that all teachers are here for you. Today, and over the next couple of weeks, we are going to support each other and take time to talk about what has happened. (CTA, 2019, ¶ 2)

RESTORATIVE CIRCLES DEPEND ON THE TRUST STUDENTS HAVE WITH OTHER MEMBERS, AND OF THE PROCESS ITSELF.

They recommended that discussion starters for these restorative circles include the following:

- What has this been like for you?
- How have you been taking care of yourself?
- How have you been taking care of others?
- Where have you seen helpers?
- How can we support each other?
- How did you help your family during or after the disaster?
- How could you help your family if you were in another disaster?
- Did anything good or positive happen because of the disaster?
- Did you learn anything?
- What has this experience made you grateful for?

This is especially important because for students to be ready to learn academic content, the emotions, concerns, or fears they are bringing with them to school must be addressed first. Keep in mind that in some instances, a teacher may need to bring in an outside facilitator to allow students to freely engage in conversation in the circle. This is especially important in instances where the teacher may be too close to the situation being discussed or can't operate as an unbiased facilitator.

Restorative circles can also be used proactively to support academic purposes. For example, in preparation for a restorative circle in a middle school social studies class, the teacher might say, "Let's first read this piece of text on the samurai tradition in feudal Japan. After reading, circle the phrase or sentence that is most significant to you. We're going to use a sequential circle to discuss our noticings." After reading, the students then share the phrase they selected, allowing for everyone to be heard. Students may even make unexpected connections with others who shared the same or similar significant phrase. The teacher then moves to a nonsequential circle to facilitate deeper discussion, using prompts such as these:

- Why were samurai well-respected in Japanese culture?

- What did the samurai value?

- What characteristics did they consider to be crucial in an ideal warrior?

- Who was left out of samurai culture? Why might this be?

Regardless of the type of circle you choose, here are some important considerations to keep in mind:

- Be strategic in how you craft the questions or discussion prompts. It is important to be specific in what you ask to avoid one-word responses.

- Be sensitive and aware of where students' responses to the questions could lead. For example, asking students to share one thing they did over the weekend can seem like a generic, community-building question. However, some students may not have had a great weekend or may have a difficult experience to share (e.g., visiting an incarcerated family member), so highlighting that experience may be painful, or you may not be prepared for how to respond.

- Have a wide range of questions available to use during restorative circles. This is important if a question you pose falls flat or to keep discussion fresh if you choose to use this strategy frequently. Questions can focus on social-emotional topics, community-building topics, academic-focused questions, concept review, current events, and more.

MANAGING BEHAVIOR IN RESTORATIVE CIRCLES

Although most students adapt well to the rhythms of a restorative circle, some problematic behavior can arise. This is often easily managed through a nonverbal signal. One recommendation is to teach two simple hand signals that can be used by any member of the group at any time (Positive Behaviour for Learning, 2014b):

- An **outstretched hand** to signal interest in speaking next

- A **raised hand** to signal that the speaker or a nonspeaker's words or actions are inconsistent with agreements

If a student persists, the circle keeper should pause the process and address the student by reminding them of the agreements and then asking them if they can abide by them. If the student says they cannot, ask them to step out of the circle and ask an adult to escort them to another area of the school. The escorting or receiving adult should use the opportunity to engage in an impromptu conversation, with the goal of returning the student to the circle, if possible.

A DILEMMA: TAKE TWO

The issue of tattling had taken over her classroom and Ms. Garcia realized that it was keeping students from learning and from their ability to work toward the beliefs and values of their class agreement. Her students had had many previous experiences with restorative circles, so gathering together now was not going to be a new process for them. Immediately upon walking back into the classroom, the teacher asks her students to engage in independent reading for 10 minutes so that she can diffuse some of the energy of the group and plan for a restorative circle. She makes a few notes to herself using part of the planning tool her school uses:

Introduction	• How will participants be welcomed? • How will the purpose of the circle be established? • Is there a need for relationship building?	• Revisit our class agreements. • "I know there are good times to tell me about something that is happening. But other times it gets in the way of how we work together. We're going to talk about how you'll know when to tell on someone." • Purpose: Are we living up to our agreement to "use kind words and help each other"?
Deepening and exploring impact	• Which questions will be asked to encourage participants to share stories? • What questions will allow participants to describe their impact? • Who has been affected and in what ways?	• "When are there good times to tell an adult about something another person is doing or saying?" • "What are your feelings when someone tattles on you?" • "What are your feelings when you are doing the telling?"

(Continued)

(Continued)

		• "Are there bad reasons to tell an adult about something another person is doing or saying?"
		• "When tattling happens for bad reasons, how do people get hurt? How does it make our learning harder?"
Repairs or actions	• How will ideas for resolution or action be shared? • How will the conversation center on healing or positive change?	• "Let's make a list of when it is a very good idea to tell an adult about something a person is doing or saying." • "Let's make another list of when it is a bad idea to tell an adult about something a person is doing or saying." • "What are some ways we can solve problems differently when we don't have a good reason for telling?"
Consensus	• How will you know that consensus has been reached? • What actions may need to be taken if consensus is not reached?	• May not reach consensus today. Might need to continue with a class meeting tomorrow to take action.

After the teacher makes some notes to herself about her plan, she invites the students to sit in a circle. She uses the stuffed animal embroidered with the school logo as their talking piece "to remind ourselves that we're thinking like Walker Wolverines." For the next 25 minutes they discuss the issue at hand as Ms. Garcia, the circle keeper, facilitates discussion using the questions she had noted. She is very happy with the T-chart they develop about good and bad reasons for telling. However, they grow more fidgety when it comes to identifying some ways to solve problems differently. "I'm not surprised," she said later. "They're five years old and this is a big topic."

She decides to begin the following day by reading *Talk and Work It Out* (Meiners, 2005) to re-engage them with the question about reaching consensus and then moves them back into a restorative circle to continue the discussion. "I'm seeing that it's going to take a series of conversations this week, but I expect that we'll have some new processes in place by the end of the week," says Ms. Garcia.

CASE IN POINT

Arturo Hernandez's geometry class has been studying scale factors of dilated polygons using quadratic equations and systems of inequalities to describe the polygons. They have a unit test on Friday, and Mr. Hernandez knows that the content has been challenging for many of his students. He also knows that the next unit relies heavily on a solid understanding of the current content, so he wants to be sure that his students really know the material.

To help him plan for the week and support his students as they prepare for the test, he decides to conduct a class circle on Monday. He plans to use a sequential circle and include the following questions:

- What is one thing you feel confident about for the test on Friday?

- What is one thing you feel unclear about or feel like you need more practice with?

Mr. Hernandez plans to base his instruction for the week on what his students share. To best meet students' needs and give them confidence going into the test on Friday, he is planning to use student feedback to create small groups for reteaching and review throughout the week.

In each of his three geometry sections that Monday, they end up using more than half the class period for the circles, which was longer than Mr. Hernandez expected. However, the students engaged in very honest conversations about what they felt confident in and what they were unclear about. A few students even offered to help others in class who were struggling with topics they felt they understood well.

Did Mr. Hernandez use class time wisely, even though he wasn't engaged in actual academic instruction? Why or why not?

RECOMMENDATIONS AND IMPLICATIONS

We have created a table of general recommendations for consideration. Add your own site-specific implications and questions that this module has provoked for you.

	BROAD RECOMMENDATIONS	SITE-SPECIFIC IMPLICATIONS AND QUESTIONS
Schoolwide	Learn about restorative circles and identify resources and professional learning opportunities to build knowledge and capacity.	
Leaders	Identify/train staff who can lead restorative circles.	
Teachers	Identify opportunities to utilize restorative circles for academic and social-emotional learning in your classroom.	
Students	Teach students about low-stakes circles to get them accustomed to the format. Co-construct agreements with them.	
Family and Community	Introduce the purposes of restorative circles and model their use in community meetings.	

REFLECTION

Let's review the success criteria from the opening of this module. Ask yourself: Can you do these things now? Write your reflections below.

Can I identify three components that are consistently used in all circles?	
Can I describe and apply the phases of a restorative circle?	
Can I compare and contrast various types of circles and decide when to use each?	

Access resources, tools, and guides
for this module at the companion website:
resources.corwin.com/restorativepracticesplaybook

MODULE 6

7

FORMAL RESTORATIVE CONFERENCES AND VICTIM-OFFENDER DIALOGUES

BELIEF STATEMENT

When serious harm occurs, school staff need procedures to process and address the incident. These procedures to process should be designed to address the needs of the victim(s) while also providing a learning opportunity for the person(s) who caused the harm.

A Dilemma

Mason is in fourth grade and is responsible for collecting sports equipment at the end of recess and putting it away. The school Mason attends rotates job responsibilities among students. At the end of recess one day, a fifth-grade student approaches Mason and tried to take a basketball away from him. This results in a verbal altercation with Mason refusing to give up the ball because recess was over and that was the rule. The other student, Finley, threatens to hurt Mason after school that day.

A teacher observes the altercation but could not hear what was said. The principal investigates and determines Finley was wrong, and that the rules indicate that the consequence of altercations during recess was to lose recess time. So, Finley is sent to the "no recess room" for the next week, where he is allowed only to draw or read during each recess break.

During the days that Finley is gone from recess, Mason becomes increasingly anxious about what might happen when Finley is allowed to return. Mason is worried that Finley will blame him and that another altercation might occur. He asks his teacher, "When does Finley get out?" Despite reassurance from his parents that everything is going to be fine, Mason counts down the days until Finley is "released."

The following week, Finley is back at recess with the other students. Finley and a group of friends corner Mason, but a teacher sees the interaction and ends it before anything happens. Mason says that Finley told him, "You better watch out. I'm gonna get you back." Finley says that he was trying to apologize to Mason. The two are sent back to class because the adults cannot determine who was correct.

After school, Mason runs all the way home. He refuses to attend school for the next several days, complaining of stomachaches and headaches. When he returns to school several days later, Mason refuses to go to recess. When forced to go, Mason stands next to an adult the entire time. Other students start calling him names and saying he is weak.

How could the school have handled this situation differently?

COMMON MISCONCEPTIONS

Misconception 1: A punishment is the best way to change behavior.

Fact: Most students do not respond to punishment in ways that result in lasting change. True change comes from taking ownership of their choices, actions, and behaviors in front of the people whose relationships mean the most to them and who are impacted by those choices, actions, and behaviors. The fear of isolation, losing a sense of belonging at school or in class, or losing the trust/relationship with those important to them has more impact than any consequence.

Misconception 2: Only administrators are involved with restorative conferences.

Fact: Administrators will likely be present for all restorative conferences, but other important adults can (and should) also be involved (e.g., sports coach if student is a player, student government advisor if student is a member of student council, or a relevant teacher or staff member), as well as the family of the student(s) involved.

Misconception 3: For most incidents, it's appropriate to go straight to a restorative conference because it gets everyone involved to help come to a resolution.

Fact: A restorative conference takes significant time and resources to conduct. While it may be the end result and may be immediately appropriate for a zero-tolerance offense, it is often more appropriate to begin with affective statements, impromptu conversations, or restorative circles to get at the root of the situation, figure out who is best to get involved, and begin finding a resolution. It may even be that a restorative conference becomes unnecessary in the situation because of the work done in advance.

Misconception 4: A restorative conference should be held right away (e.g., 30 minutes later or the next day) after an incident.

Fact: It is important not to let too much time go between the time of the incident and the conference. However, more important is that everyone involved has some time to process, can calm down if necessary, and figure out who is essential for the conversation to have the most impact. For example, if it's discovered that a parent is a major component in the incident, but they're on a work trip, it may be necessary to wait until they are back in town.

Misconception 5: "I have a restorative mindset. That's all I need to facilitate restorative conferences."

Fact: Because formal restorative conferences are reserved for more serious incidents, training is key. People who facilitate formal restorative conferences should receive training on how to do so. However, your restorative mindset plays an important part when you are a participant.

LEARNING INTENTIONS

- I am learning about high-stakes conferences that address serious harm.
- I am learning about consequences and accountability following harm.

SUCCESS CRITERIA

- I can describe the various roles that individuals play in restorative conferences.
- I can identify ways in which I can participate in restorative conferences.
- I can explain the ways in which accountability, consequences, and transformation can occur.
- I can participate in re-entry conversations and actions.

SELF-ASSESSMENT

Directions: Unlike the other modules in this book, restorative conferences and victim-offender dialogue sessions are facilitated by people with more advanced training and experiences. Importantly, the success of these high-stakes conversations rests on the effective implementation of a restorative culture and the regular interactions that teachers and staff have with students, and that students have with peers. For this self-assessment, reflect on the experiences that students and staff have in school.

CONDITION	IN PLACE	PARTIALLY IN PLACE	NOT IN PLACE
School staff receive regular professional learning opportunities to expand their knowledge of restorative practices.			
School staff have clear definitions for behaviors that interfere with academic and social success.			

CONDITION	IN PLACE	PARTIALLY IN PLACE	NOT IN PLACE
School staff have agreed upon, and documented, which classroom behaviors are managed through classroom-based restorative practices strategies and which behaviors are office managed, including when a behavior requires a restorative *conference*.			
Written orientation information on restorative practices is available for all volunteers, substitute teachers, and guest teachers who will be interacting with students.			
Circles are a regularly occurring event in classrooms.			
School staff have agreed upon and documented which types and severity of behavioral incidents will be addressed by the teacher alone in the classroom, and which behavioral incidents require co-facilitation of circle.			
School staff use informal restorative *conversations* in response to situations, as agreed.			
School staff use informal restorative *conferences* in response to situations, as agreed.			
Processes have been defined for follow-up meetings to restorative conferencing.			
Follow-up meetings include all participants to make sure agreement had been followed and to discuss anything else that has come up since the initial conference.			
School team(s) assess fidelity of restorative practices at least once per quarter.			
School team(s) review outcome data (suspensions, attendance, restorative practices surveys, climate surveys, etc.) at least once per quarter.			

Source: Illinois Balanced and Restorative Justice (n.d.).

PEOPLE WHO FACILITATE FORMAL RESTORATIVE CONFERENCES SHOULD RECEIVE TRAINING ON HOW TO DO SO.

Formal restorative conferences get a lot of attention, although in practice they occur far less often than the affective statements, impromptu conversations, and restorative circles discussed in previous modules. These formal restorative conferences reflect the influence of restorative justice, as these are reserved for serious offenses that cause great physical, psychological, and emotional harm. In many cases, they encompass infractions outlined in district and state code of conduct policies. The nature of the infraction may involve law enforcement.

One myth that persists is that there is an either/or decision when it comes to addressing serious infractions. In other words, either you engage in a formal restorative conference, *or* you suspend and expel. This was expressed by a visitor interested in restorative practices at the school where we work, who told Dominique, "I came to see your Hug-a-Thug program." It remains one of the most offensive remarks we have witnessed and says as much about the person who uttered it as it does about a major misconception regarding restorative practices. Serious infractions often warrant punishment. But punishment alone does not change behavior, which is why psychologists, behavior specialists, and criminal justice experts pair it with teaching and reinforcement.

The United Nations Office on Crime and Drugs supports formal restorative conferences as a part of a restorative justice approach when three conditions are met:

1. The offender must accept or not deny responsibility for the incident.

2. Both the victim and the offender must be willing to participate.

3. Both the victim and the offender must consider it safe to be involved in the process.

The purpose of a formal restorative conference is not to weigh blame. It is not a forum for assessing the situation to determine who is at fault. That determination is made in advance, using processes outlined by the school district, and, if applicable, by the criminal justice system. However, a formal restorative conference is an option available to use after that determination is made.

There are sound reasons for utilizing formal restorative conferences as part of a response to an incident that has caused serious harm. Among the strongest arguments is to counter the school-to-prison pipeline that negatively impacts BIPOC youth (Darby, 2021; Fronius et al., 2019). To be clear, the number of incidents that require involvement with the criminal justice system is small but significant in terms of its impact on the entire school community. The intent, however, is to provide a forum for victims and offenders to address the impact of the harm and to give each the opportunity to receive closure (see Figure 7.1).

While formal restorative conferences are less common at school, they do occur. For the purposes of the remainder of the module, we'll confine our discussion to serious incidents that do not extensively involve the criminal justice system. Local law enforcement and juvenile justice systems have their own procedures that govern their formal involvement in restorative justice that are beyond the scope of this book. To learn more about efforts in your area, contact your local juvenile justice agency and your district.

Figure 7.1 Common Attributes of Restorative Justice Programs	
VICTIMS ARE PROVIDED WITH AN OPPORTUNITY TO . . .	**OFFENDERS ARE PROVIDED WITH AN OPPORTUNITY TO . . .**
• Be directly involved in resolving the situation and addressing the consequences of the offense.	• Acknowledge responsibility for the offense and understand the effects of the offense on the victim.
• Receive answers to their questions about the crime and the offender.	• Express emotions (even remorse) about the offense.
• Express themselves about the impact of the offense.	• Receive support to repair harm caused to the victim or oneself and family.
• Receive restitution or reparation.	• Make amends or restitution/reparation.
• Receive an apology.	• Apologize to victims.
• Restore, when appropriate, a relationship with the offender.	• Restore their relationship with the victim when appropriate.
• Reach closure.	• Reach closure.

Source: United Nations Office on Drugs and Crime (2006).

Reread your own writing in Module 1, where you reflected on your experiences as a victim and as an offender (pages 15–16). How has your thinking evolved? What has remained constant?

SCHOOL-BASED FORMAL RESTORATIVE CONFERENCES

Some serious infractions that involve school-based formal restorative conferences fall into a gray area that affords schools the discretion to address it entirely on their own, such as underage drinking, bullying, cyberbullying, and fights that do not result in serious injuries. Other incidents are entirely under the purview of the school, such as chronic attendance problems, smoking, and violations of the school honor code.

These conferences adhere to the same tenets as those outlined by the UN:

- The offender has accepted or does not deny responsibility in the incident.

- Victims and offenders mutually agree to engage in the process.

- Both feel safe in doing so.

The goal of school-based formal restorative conferences is to help students take ownership of their actions, choices, and behaviors and realize the impact those actions, choices, and behaviors have beyond themselves. For restorative work to be effective, you as the teacher have to be willing to engage in discussion with students around those topics, even if it's hard and uncomfortable, to come to a resolution that can assist the young people involved in growing and learning from the event.

THE GOAL OF SCHOOL-BASED FORMAL RESTORATIVE CONFERENCES IS TO HELP STUDENTS TAKE OWNERSHIP OF THEIR ACTIONS AND REALIZE THE IMPACT THOSE ACTIONS HAVE BEYOND THEMSELVES.

As with other dimensions of formal restorative conferences, the facilitator involved has been trained to do so. Holding an administrative or counseling position at a school isn't sufficient. We encourage you not to wade into these waters without more intensive professional development and reading. However, we do want to equip you with information about what a range of these conferences looks like.

Even within the frame of school-based formal restorative conferences, there is a range of customs that should be considered on a case-by-case basis. We'll begin with a high-stakes example. In these cases, victims and offenders are invited to bring supporters to be able to articulate the impact on them. They are not there to argue the case but rather to deepen the perspectives on how harm has occurred. The planning tool in Figure 7.2 can serve as a guide for ensuring that the conference doesn't devolve into a "they said/they said" spiral.

Figure 7.2 Planning Tool for Formal School-Based Restorative Conferences

PHASE	SCRIPT	NOTES
Introductions	Welcome. I am (your name) and I will be the facilitator for this conference. Could you each introduce yourself and let us know your relationship to the others in this room?	
Setting the stage	Thank you all for being here. I understand that this is difficult, and I know that your presence here will help us address the situation (or incident). This is an opportunity for all of you to be involved in repairing the harm that has been done.	
	This conference will focus on an incident that happened (share the date, setting, and nature of the event but refrain from elaborating).	
	It is important that we focus on what (offender name[s]) did and how that has impacted others. We are not here to decide if they are good or bad. We want to focus on how people have been impacted and work to repair the harm that has occurred. Does everyone understand and agree?	
	(Offender name[s]) has/have admitted to their part in the incident. We are not here to decide on guilt or innocence.	
	Directed to offender(s): You are not required to participate in this conference. You can leave at any time. If you do leave, the administrative team will make decisions about the course of action.	
	Directed to all other participants: You are not required to participate in this conference. You can leave at any time. If you do, we will continue to work through the harm and attempt to reach some decisions.	

(Continued)

MODULE 7

(Continued)

PHASE	SCRIPT	NOTES
Offender(s)	We will start with (one offender's name). If there is more than one, each will respond to the following questions: • What happened? • What were you thinking about at the time? • What have you thought about since the incident? • Who do you think has been affected by your actions? • How have they been impacted?	
Victim(s)	We will start with (one victim's name). If there is more than one, each will respond to the following questions: • What was your reaction at the time of the incident? • How do you feel about what happened? • What has been the hardest thing for you? • How did your family and friends react when they heard about the incident?	
Victim supporters	Each supporter responds to all the following questions: • What did you think when you heard about this incident? • How do you feel about what happened? • What has been the hardest thing for you? • What do you think are the main issues?	

PHASE	SCRIPT	NOTES
Offender supporters	For the parent/caregiver: This has been difficult for you, hasn't it? What would you like to tell us about it?	
	All offender supporters respond to the following questions: • What did you think when you heard about this incident? • How do you feel about what happened? • What has been the hardest thing for you? • What do you think are the main issues?	
Offender(s)	Is there anything you want to say at this time?	
Identifying needs	Ask the victim(s): What would you like from today's conference?	
	Invite offender(s) to respond to each suggestion before moving to the next.	
	(As agreement develops, clarify each item. Keep a written record with details, deadlines, and follow-up agreements.)	
Reaching agreements	(As the agreements are finalized and the meeting is starting to end) Before I finalize our agreements, I would like to make sure that I have things recorded correctly. I want to be sure that I didn't leave out any details about what has been decided.	
	(Read agreements and look for acknowledgment.)	
Closure	Before we end this conference, I would like to provide everyone with a final opportunity to speak. Is there anything anyone wants to say?	
	Thank you all for your contributions today. We are dealing with a difficult situation, and we have been able to work through many issues. Congratulations on the way you have supported each other. Have some refreshments while I finalize the agreement.	

Source: Adapted from Wachtel et al. (2010). Copyright © International Institute for Restorative Practices. All rights reserved. Used with permission.

MODULE 7

A SCHOOL-BASED FORMAL CONFERENCE: ALCOHOL CONSUMPTION AT SCHOOL

Emery enrolls in a new school as an eleventh grader. Throughout the first week, students are grouped across grade levels and rotate through a series of tasks that include culture-building activities, academic screening assessments, signing up for internships, and logistics such as getting identification cards, signing out technology and books, and reviewing the student handbook that is developed each year in partnership with the student government group. The groups stay together for the week and each group has a faculty advisor. On the final day of that first week, the entire study body is transported to a local park for a series of team-building activities. The various groups compete for spirit points during the team-building activities.

The goal of this week is to re-establish the culture of the school, establish expectations, and identify students who may need supplemental academic support before too many weeks of instruction have occurred. But this is just context for what happens next: during the culture-building day, Emery gets drunk. Emery takes a bottle of alcohol on the bus and goes into a public bathroom to drink. His teacher for the week notices this behavior and the smell of alcohol on his breath. The principal is contacted and meets with Emery. Emery admits to drinking and is stumbling and slurring his words. The principal calls Emery's stepmother, who leaves work to come to the park. When Emery's stepmom arrives, she decides it's time for Emery to go home under her supervision. Obviously, there's no point in having a conference with someone who has been drinking.

The following Monday, Emery's advisory teacher, several students from the group, the student government president, the principal, Emery, and Emery's stepmother are invited into a school-based formal restorative conference. There was no question that Emery had been drinking—the conference is not about litigating whether he had or had not, as he had already admitted it. Emery's stepmother, as his supporter, has been prepared in advance for the conference so that she is aware of the process and her role.

Emery talks about the stress of attending school and reveals that this was the first time in more than 15 months that he had been on a school campus. As Emery says, "I didn't go to school at all last year. And I was kicked out in ninth grade for fighting and I just never went back. My cousin goes to school here and told me how good it was. So, I decided to try. But it's hard, you know? I feel stupid and I'm behind in credits to graduate. I don't want to be that person that is left after everyone else graduates."

The conversation continues and the victims have a chance to speak. The teacher says, "I was really scared. And I didn't feel like I did my job. I'm supposed to keep you all safe. And I didn't. You got drunk on my watch and I feel really bad about it."

One of the peers says, "I'm angry. We were supposed to be working as a team. And we didn't get our advisor because he had to be watching you. That's not fair to us. It's not that we lost, but that we missed out on this experience. And this is my last year here, and it was supposed to be a memory."

Each person has their say, including Emery's stepmother. She says, "I love you. And your dad loves you. He couldn't come because he's afraid that you will make the same mistakes he made. It's too painful for him. He's clean now, but it was really hard. I took off work to get you at the park because I was so scared. I want a great life for you, and I just hope this school doesn't kick you out. You need an education. I know that you want to be somebody. How can we help you? Your dad and I will do whatever you need. We love you so much."

As you can imagine, Emery is in tears for most of the meeting. There are a series of agreements reached, including drug counseling, peer mediation, making amends, and such. At the end of the meeting, Emery says to the advisory teacher, "Thanks for not giving up on me. I didn't mean to make you look bad or hurt your feelings. I'm going to make it right. You'll never have another problem from me again." True to the words spoken, Emery never was an offender again and he graduated from high school the following year.

Not all meetings are as smooth as this one. And sometimes, students make additional mistakes and need several restorative conferences to learn that their actions impact others. We did not focus on the decisions or "consequences" in this section, but we will later in this module. In this section, we wanted to focus on the process and the ways in which people work toward agreements and making amends. What if Emery had been drinking again? Or engaged in some other offense? Would that mean that the restorative conference failed? Or would we see it as a process and, as part of that process, the people who were hurt had their say and reached closure?

COMPARE AND CONTRAST WRITTEN REFLECTION

Consider an infraction that has occurred at your site—one that did not involve law enforcement but caused serious harm. Compare and contrast ways in which a punitive approach to the incident would differ from a restorative one.

THREE QUESTIONS PUNITIVE PRACTICES ASK	THREE QUESTIONS RESTORATIVE PRACTICES ASK
What law or rule was broken?	What is the harm caused by this action?
Who broke it?	What are the needs and obligations of all affected by the harm?
What punishment is deserved?	How can all the affected parties create a plan to heal the harm as much as possible?

Source: Adapted from Oakland Unified School District (n.d.).

WHAT DOES THIS LOOK LIKE FOR YOUNG CHILDREN?

There are times when serious incidents occur in the primary grades. Many of us have read about the policing of young children who have had a violent outburst at school. Rather than working with the child and the family, law enforcement is called to arrest the child. The sight of a five-year-old in handcuffs is chilling. Students with disabilities, especially those who have cognitive and behavioral disabilities, are also at higher risk. Yet it continues to happen at schools around the country. Schools that see no alternative other than law enforcement have a serious capacity gap that increases the risk for every child at that school.

Educators who work with young children and with people with intellectual disabilities are eager to use restorative conferencing but may struggle with how to use a process that is developmentally appropriate. Using a script adapted for young children (see Figure 7.3), the early childhood and primary grades staff at Garcia Elementary School help young children resolve serious infractions in ways that are growth-producing.

For example, Evan, a four-year-old in a transitional kindergarten class, has a violent temper tantrum in his class one morning. Angry with a classmate over a glue bottle they were supposed to share, Evan hits his peer and kicks over the chair. Kace Carter, the teacher, attempts to intervene to calm the child down and remove him safely from the area. However, this enrages Evan, who then pelts the teacher with nearby objects, including a large metal stapler. Ms. Carter needs three stitches to close the laceration on her forehead. Fortunately, the school has a crisis intervention response, and Evan is sent home for the day in the company of a parent, who is horrified and ashamed to hear what had happened.

SCHOOLS THAT SEE NO ALTERNATIVE OTHER THAN LAW ENFORCEMENT HAVE A SERIOUS CAPACITY GAP THAT INCREASES THE RISK FOR EVERY CHILD AT THAT SCHOOL.

Shawn Latrelle, the school's restorative practices coordinator, contacts the family to let them know about a restorative conference they would like to hold between Evan and the teacher. Mr. Latrelle prepares the family by discussing the purpose of the meeting and the desired outcomes. "It's crucial to also hear the family's worries and concerns," he explains to them. They discuss possible follow-up interventions, including work with the school counselor on anger management. Mr. Latrelle also meets with the teacher to hear her concerns and emotions. "Ms. Carter was great, but you can't just expect people to bear an event like that and just go on. She needed to be able to share her feelings with me, so she could be in a better place for Evan."

The following morning, Evan arrives at school with his family. He is greeted warmly by Mr. Latrelle and the facilitator as well as by the principal and the teacher. ("You could already see the relief in his eyes," Mr. Latrelle later remarked.) Using the script to frame the conference, Mr. Latrelle leads Evan through the process while his family and his teacher watch. He occasionally invites them into the conversation. As part of the agreements, Mr. Latrelle tells Evan that the school counselor will also be meeting with him weekly "to give you better tools to use when you're angry." Evan apologizes to his teacher, who accepts his apology.

"I'll use a similar process with Evan and the student he hit after he has a morning snack. It will be more low-key and shorter," says the facilitator. "Just me and the two of them." Ms. Carter tells Evan's parents, "Our goal is to get him back into a learning state as soon as possible. But I want to thank you for your support of Evan and me. We make a good team."

Figure 7.3 Early Years Script for Restorative Conferences

Tell the story.	What happened? When you _____, was that a good choice or a bad choice?
Explore the harm.	How do you think _____ felt when you _____?
Repair the harm.	To fix this, you need to _____.
Reach an agreement.	At school it's not okay to _____. How can we make sure this doesn't happen again?
Plan follow-up.	I'm going to check in on you later to see that you're doing what we agreed. What do you think we should do if something like this happens again?
Give the apology (if appropriate).	**The person who caused the harm** I'm sorry/I apologize for _____. I was _____ because _____. **The person who has been harmed** I didn't like it when you _____. It made me feel _____. Thank you for your apology.

Source: Langley (2016).

STEPPING INTO THE DISPUTE: WHEN THEY BOTH MIGHT BE AT FAULT

Sometimes it is difficult to figure out who has done harm (the offender) and who has been harmed (the victim) in a situation (e.g., Student A only fought Student B during lunch because Student B had pushed them and said an insult to them earlier in the day). Disputes between students often have contributing factors that each of them needs to own. Because of this, multiple restorative conferences may need to occur to resolve the situation and allow for both students to see the impact of their behaviors. In the fight example, a series of conversations may need to occur separately with each student before bringing the students involved together at the same time for a formal restorative conference. This is an opportunity to do the prework needed to get them ready. It is also a chance to investigate a bit further to assess the conflict. For instance, is the fight the result of bullying that has gone undetected?

It is useful to broker dialogue between the students to reach a resolution. In cases where the lines between victim and offender are blurred, the goal is less about assigning blame wholly to one party or the other, but rather to assist each in recognizing the impact of their actions, and to move them to resolution. In keeping with central principles of restorative practices, use questions like those featured in the planning tool, as they are designed to surface the reflective thinking of the individuals. Figure 7.4 contains questions to use to engage in restorative conferencing.

Figure 7.4 Victim and Offender Questions

QUESTIONS TO ASK THE PERSON WHO HAS DONE HARM	QUESTIONS TO ASK THE PERSON WHO HAS BEEN HARMED
• What happened? • What were you thinking about at the time of the incident? • What have you thought about since the incident? • Who has been affected by what you've done? In what way? • What do you think you need to do to make things right?	• What did you think when you realized what happened? • What impact has this incident had on you and others? • What has been the hardest on you? • What do you think needs to be done to make things right?

Source:

When we ask these questions, we want to hear their perspectives of the situation to see whether there is some underlying cause or trigger that can be addressed and what was really going through their mind leading up to, during, and after the time of the incident. We also want to help the student understand that their actions have an impact on more than just themselves, and by confronting those individuals during a restorative conference we open the door to rebuilding the relationships that may have been damaged or changed as a result of the incident. When asked about what needs to happen to make things right, the students are often harder on themselves than the typical consequence would have been. By allowing them input into the resolution of the incident, everyone involved can begin to heal.

We also want to hear from their perspectives in terms of the harm they suffered because of the incident. This can help identify additional causes or triggers for the situation as well as to consider a perspective they may not have understood previously. When asked about what needs to happen to make things right, often the student is willing to extend grace to the other through a reasonable resolution. We are educators, and we want to hold a space for students to learn

MODULE 7

about themselves, about others, and how to address future situations differently. When we bring the students together, we allow them to state their responses to the questions (as victim and as offender) so that they can gain the perspectives of the other. We add four further questions to pose jointly to the students:

1. What do you know now that you wished you had known then?

2. If a similar situation were to occur, what would you do differently?

3. What commitments for resolution are you willing to make to move forward?

4. What is our plan for checking in for follow-up?

WHEN ASKED ABOUT WHAT NEEDS TO HAPPEN TO MAKE THINGS RIGHT, THE STUDENTS ARE OFTEN HARDER ON THEMSELVES THAN THE TYPICAL CONSEQUENCE WOULD HAVE BEEN.

You may find yourself involved in a school-based restorative conference that is led by a trained facilitator. It is important to be self-aware, as your involvement probably means you were involved or impacted by the incident. Consider the preparation techniques you will use to remain restorative and to allow it to be a restorative conference, not a "restorative lecture."

How will I process my own emotions in advance of the conference?	
How will I maintain my role as an active listener?	
What do I need to do, and avoid, in my body language?	
How will I process my own emotions after the conference?	

DECISIONS AND CONSEQUENCES

Actions have reactions, and too often, the reactions in schools are punitive and exclusionary. Having said that, it's important to note that there are usually consequences that result from formal restorative conferences. There are also consequences when a student does not want to participate in a restorative conference. We have lost count of the number of times a student has asked us, "Can't you just suspend me?" To which we respond, "Of course we can, but you'd miss the opportunity to learn."

Sometimes, schools and school systems have specific guidelines for actions that must be taken in specific situations. If that is the case, teams will probably need to follow those guidelines and, at the same time, work with leaders to update the policies. Irrespective of the consequences imposed by others, it is important to explore the suggestions made by the victims, offenders, and supporters. They have good ideas, and they know what they need to move forward. And students are more willing to accept the consequences if they feel their voice is being heard. If there are non-negotiable consequences, discuss them in the group and note why they have been put in place. Offenders, victims, and supporters should not be surprised that, after a productive conversation, there are additional actions that leaders will take.

STUDENTS ARE MORE WILLING TO ACCEPT THE CONSEQUENCES IF THEY FEEL THEIR VOICE IS BEING HEARD.

We are often asked about suspension as a consequence for seriously harmful actions. There really isn't evidence that it's the suspension that changes student behavior. Punitive actions don't accomplish that. But consequences, which include accountability to the organization, the community, and oneself, do change student behavior. Three days' banishment from school doesn't do that.

But we know there are times when a cool-off period is appropriate. After a fight, for example, the various parties may need to be away from school to gain some perspective before engaging in a formal restorative conference. We recognize that it's easy to say "Don't suspend students," especially by people who are not in schools every day. But we are realists, and we recognize that there are times that school teams will make this decision and they should not be shamed for their actions. We just ask that teams track the decisions they make and monitor the differential application of exclusionary practices on certain groups of students. The evidence suggests that BIPOC students and those with disabilities are suspended at much higher rates, often for the same offenses as their white, Asian, or nondisabled peers.

Often, it's the grown-ups who need a cooling-off period. When serious things happen on our campuses, we are hurt and angry, and we tend to take more extreme positions. When we have time to cool off and listen to the various perspectives of others (including the offender), we are much more likely to make wise and growth-producing decisions. Restorative practices are easy to watch from a distance. We may even become cheerleaders for the work. But when the situation impacts us, we all tend to shift back to punitive actions. Again, a cool-off period may be needed so we can collectively revisit why restorative practices are important.

Having said that, every one of us has recommended the suspension of a student. Sometimes, this can be accomplished with the student remaining on campus, perhaps with several check-ins with counselors or social workers. However, it may be necessary for the student to go home. But let's not fool ourselves into believing that the exclusionary practice is going to result in behavior change. Regardless of whether the team decides on a suspension, there should be other decisions that the team makes.

THE JUSTICE MODEL OF CIRCLE SENTENCING

One process that is growing in popularity within restorative groups is based on the justice model of circle sentencing. There are four stages to this process:

Stage 1: Determining whether the specific case is suitable for a circle process

Stage 2: Preparing the parties that will be involved in the circle

Stage 3: Seeking a consensual agreement in the circle

Stage 4: Providing follow-up and ensuring the offender adheres to the agreement

The comparison forwarded by the criminal justice system highlights the differences.

CRIMINAL COURT	COMMUNITY SENTENCING CIRCLES
• Regards the conflict as the crime	• Regards the criminal incident as a small part of a larger dynamic/conflict
• Sees the sentence as resolving the conflict	• Sees the sentence as a small part of the solution
• Focuses on past conduct	• Focuses on present and future conduct
• Takes a narrow view of behavior	• Takes a larger, holistic view
• Victim(s) may receive an apology	
• Avoids broader concern with social conflict	• Focuses on social conflict
• Considers the result (i.e., the sentence) most important	• Considers the result least important—the process is most important, as the process shapes and sometimes heals the relationships among parties
• Relies on professionals	• Empowers the community

Source: Adapted from B. D. Stuart in Griffiths & Cunningham (2007, p. 271).

In contrast to the formal and often adversarial approach to justice, circle sentencing can help

- Reacquaint individuals, families, and communities with problem-solving skills.

- Rebuild relationships within communities.

- Promote awareness and respect for values and the lives of others.

- Address the needs and interests of all parties, including the victim.

- Focus action on causes, not just symptoms, of problems.

- Recognize existing healing resources and create new ones.

- Coordinate the use of local and government resources.

- Generate preventive measures. (United Nations Office on Drugs and Crime, 2006)

Azariah agrees to participate in a version of a sentencing circle as a result of stealing from a middle school classroom. Azariah was caught with the items (phones, tablets, computers) at home and was not contesting the fact that they were stolen. The phones were returned to their owners and the other equipment was returned to the school. The victim is represented by the principal and the decision was made to use a modified justice sentencing circle. The team decides not to have a restorative conference but rather focus on the actions that would occur because of the thievery.

At this school, they call the process ACT (accountability, consequences, and transformation). "We wanted this process to reflect our restorative culture," says principal Ellis Long. "Each of these words represents our intention that there is student accountability paired with what happens afterward—the consequences." He continues, "But it all needs to build a path toward transformation for the student." Team members change, depending on the situation and the people involved, but there is usually an ACT team leader who is part of the process each time.

The ACT team consists of Azariah's dad, two peers, the teacher, and the school social worker. This group makes recommendations to the administrative team. At this school, and many others, recommendations are made to another group who makes the final decision, in part based on policies, educational codes and regulations, and experience. It's very common for the student, and sometimes the others in the meeting, to recommend much more serious consequences and they may need to be toned down a bit.

The recommendations made on behalf of Azariah include the following:

- Written apologies to all peers involved, with a commitment not to repeat the offense

- Working in the technology center to re-install software that had been erased

- A restorative conference with the teacher who was stolen from

- Daily counseling with the social worker to address underlying issues until recommended to reduce or discontinue

- Bedroom checks by the family to determine if there were items not belonging to Azariah

The leadership team meet to review the recommendations and agree to them. They also want to have a conversation with Azariah and hear directly from the student about the impact of this experience, including the process the school used to resolve the actions.

RE-ENTRY PLANS

Regardless of a suspension or not, when there is a decision to hold a restorative conference, there needs to be a re-entry plan. The student has been out of the normal flow of the classroom and school, and lots of people (peers and staff) have likely noticed. Naturally, people are curious and want to know *What happened?* They are really asking, *What punishments did the offender receive?* At the outset of the restorative practices journey, this question will be raised often. And it will be raised by students, teachers, staff, and family members. It's natural because that's what we have experienced in our pasts. Over time, members of the school community realize that the decisions that are made during restorative conferences are powerful and that there are consequences that do not rely on punitive actions.

RE-ENTRY PLANS HELP PARTICIPANTS PREPARE FOR THE EXPERIENCE OF RETURNING TO THE LEARNING ENVIRONMENT.

In reality, only the individuals impacted by the events deserve to know the course of action that has been decided. Both victims and offenders still have rights, and privacy is one of those rights. But reality comes into play. It's awkward for those involved in restorative conferences to re-enter the learning environment. When people feel awkward, they tend to either over-share or go silent. We have even had students exaggerate the consequences so that their peers think that bad things happened. As one student told us, "I did something bad, and I wanted them to know I was punished." When asked why, this student responded, "Well, I don't think that they'll understand what I committed to do and why that's even more powerful." It just reminded us that we need to create a restorative culture and change the narrative about punishments.

Re-entry plans help participants prepare for the experience of returning to the learning environment. And re-entry plans are not limited to the offenders. If the victims, supporters, and bystanders are not part of the re-entry plan, wounds may be reopened and conflict will re-ignite. Figure 7.5 contains suggested ideas for re-entry plans.

Figure 7.5 Planning Re-Entry

1. **Rehearse with the student.** Discuss with the student how he or she might respond to different scenarios upon returning to the learning environment. We like to practice with students using phrases such as "It's okay now" or "It's over now" to help offenders respond to prying questions from classmates.

2. **Identify a lifeline if needed.** Students returning to class or school from an emotionally charged event may find themselves more anxious or uneasy than anticipated. In such cases, educators should work with them to identify a "lifeline" they might use in case they need to take a short break upon their return.

3. **Schedule short follow-up intervals and adhere to them.** Checking in with students once or twice a day after they've returned from an imposed absence can help to anchor their days and gives students a safety valve.

4. **Close the loop with the adults involved so that they can more effectively respond to students' emotions.** Teachers may have unrealistic expectations for students who have been removed from the instructional flow, assuming they'll be able to pick up right where they left off. Educators in charge of students' re-entry plans should escort their students back to class on their return so that they can apprise teachers of both the students' current state of mind and of the commitments they've made.

5. **Arrange an end-of-day check-in.** These types of follow-ups can provide students with the excuse they need to peel away from friends who might otherwise escalate their misbehavior. They also give educators one more opportunity to provide students with guidance and positive affirmations.

6. **Implement the follow-up plan.** Long-term change can only be realized when students are able to truly reflect on the harm they've caused and what they've learned since. We are not suggesting that students be forced to dwell on the past forever, but regular follow-up conversations following a major event can reduce reoccurrence and build stronger relationships between students and adults.

Source: Smith et al. (2015).

INVOLVING PARENTS IN RE-ENTRY

The Governor's Office in Washington state developed a set of questions that they recommend be used with families before a student re-enters the school following a suspension. Their possible discussion questions include

- What is your student's perspective on what happened? What is the school's perspective on what happened?

- How might your student make amends (repair damage to things or relationships)?

- How might the school support better outcomes and/or repair the relationships between the school (staff) and your student and you?

MODULE 7

- What is the safety plan for the future that does its best to honor the dignity of your student, your family, and the staff of the school?

- How will your student reconnect academically and socially at school to aim toward success?

- How/when will the administrator follow up with you and your student? (Washington State Governor's Office of the Education Ombuds, n.d.)

Again, the point is to have a plan in place so that success is more likely to be the result of the restorative conference.

A DILEMMA: TAKE TWO

Let's revisit the recess scenario between Mason and Finley. The entire situation could have been resolved differently had a school-based restorative conference been used—the first opportunity came after the initial incident and could have prevented the second incident from occurring altogether.

The principal wasn't privy to the threat Finley made, and the dispute initially looked like one where there wasn't a clear victim and offender. But initial meetings with each child, using the questions to pose outlined on page 143, might have uncovered the true nature of the incident. Once identified, work with each child begins. For Mason, it is a discussion about what he needs. For Finley, it is a discussion about his thinking at the time and now. In both cases, the purpose is to provoke reflective thinking. Once that has occurred, it is time to offer a restorative conference as a choice. Again, keep in mind that both parties need to agree: the outcome should be mutually beneficial. Instead of isolating Finley and taking away a healthy outlet for energy, Finley could have been given the opportunity to recognize how the behavior affected Mason and apologize for hitting him. And Mason would have had the opportunity to have closure on the situation without fear of retaliation and avoided a period of significant anxiety.

 ## CASE IN POINT

As part of a field trip, a group of high school students goes on a tour of the University of California, Los Angeles (UCLA). While there, they visit the campus bookstore. Martina tries to steal a handful of logoed pens and gets caught by security. The security officer takes Martina to one of the chaperoning teachers and explains the situation. The guard then goes on to say that Martina is banned from the campus and that the high school is also not welcome to return.

When Martina and the other students return to school, she sits down with the principal to discuss what happened using the questioning methods of a restorative conference. Martina explains that she just really had wanted the pens but felt terrible that her mom was ashamed and that she cost the high school the opportunity to ever return to UCLA's campus.

When asked by the principal what she needs to do to make it right, Martina begins to share more about the real reason she stole the pens. She further explains that even though she's from a poor neighborhood in San Diego and people have always told her she couldn't do it, she really wants to attend school at UCLA. She says that she stole the pens because she knew that in order to go to UCLA she needed to learn to speak and write well, and if she used those pens as she wrote in school, it would remind her to work hard and never give up on her goal. She explains that she has been working and saving her money, and she plans to spend some of that money on writing supplies for her brother's third-grade classroom. She decides to donate the writing materials and share her experience with her brother's class to make sure they understood that you don't have to steal and that no matter where you're from, you can make it.

In addition, she decides to write a letter of apology to the university president and explain the entire situation. The university president personally writes a letter back to Martina, thanking her for her honesty. He also explains that the security guard had no authority to ban her or her high school from UCLA's campus and that, based on her integrity, students from her high school are welcome any time. With his letter, he also includes a whole box of UCLA-branded pens.

What effect do you think the restorative conference had on the outcome of Martina's choices? Had a more traditional consequence approach been taken to this situation, do you think the same outcome would have been produced?

RECOMMENDATIONS AND IMPLICATIONS

We have created a table of general recommendations for consideration. Add your own site-specific implications and questions that this module has provoked for you.

	BROAD RECOMMENDATIONS	SITE-SPECIFIC IMPLICATIONS AND QUESTIONS
Schoolwide	Examine the previous three years of suspensions and expulsions for racial, ethnic, gender, and disability disparities. Compare outcomes across similar incidents. Do disparities exist for similar infractions?	
Leaders	Identify a task force of key representatives from the school community, including students and families, to gather information about formal restorative conferences. Should this be a part of your site's efforts for restorative practices?	
Teachers	Meet as colleagues to develop a description of the roles and responsibilities of classroom teachers as participants (not as facilitators) in the process.	
Students	Work with student representatives to explore their interest in developing systems for school-based restorative conferences.	
Family and Community	Work with community leaders and law enforcement to determine resources and needs for putting formal restorative conferences in place.	

REFLECTION

Let's review the success criteria from the opening of this module. Ask yourself: Can you do these things now? Write your reflections below.

Can I describe the various roles that individuals play in restorative conferences?	
Can I identify ways in which I can participate in restorative conferences?	
Can I explain the ways in which accountability, consequences, and transformation can occur?	
Can I participate in re-entry conversations and actions?	

Access resources, tools, and guides
for this module at the companion website:
resources.corwin.com/restorativepracticesplaybook

WHAT DOES SUCCESS LOOK LIKE?

"But does it work?"

How many times have we been asked this question? We understand people want to find something that works because what many schools are doing now simply does not work. Harm remains and long-term change is not happening. We have included a number of studies throughout this playbook that have highlighted the impact that restorative justice and restorative practices can have.

But restorative practices are often held to an unrealistic standard. If the student does something egregious again, doubt is cast on the process. But is the same standard applied to public humiliation techniques, such as clip charts and names on the board, and suspension or other exclusionary practices? How many times have we heard that a specific student has been suspended five times? Or that a child has been on the lowest level of the behavior chart for months?

Restorative practices are not a quick fix. If you want immediate compliance, there are faster ways to get temporary changes. If the goal is to remove a student from the school environment so you can get some temporary peace, a suspension is more efficient. But if you want students to understand their impact and to develop prosocial skills that serve them well as they enter the community, restorative practices are for you. Now that you're familiar with the evidence and practices, we'll share one of many success stories. In this case, we did not change the name. This is a real person who shared his story so that others could benefit. Meet Uriel Cortez, soon to hold a master's degree in marriage and family therapy. But we get ahead of ourselves.

> HE FULLY EXPECTED THAT IT WAS ONLY A MATTER OF TIME BEFORE HE WAS SUSPENDED, OR MAYBE EVEN EXPELLED, FROM HIS NEW HIGH SCHOOL.

URIEL'S STORY

Growing up, Uriel attended elementary and middle schools that took a traditional approach to discipline. When he exhibited negative behaviors, he experienced consequences such as clip charts, classroom removal, referrals, and suspensions.

Although he liked math and science, he didn't experience much academic success and, over time, turned to the influence of his extended family and joined a gang. "I never really wanted to be in a gang; it was just sort of expected of me," he said. "I was interested in a lot of things growing up—soccer, sports, medicine—but because of where I came from, you couldn't express yourself like that. It was considered a weakness, and you could get preyed on for that."

In middle school, Uriel learned how to play the part of a hardened gang member. He dressed, spoke, and acted tough and didn't put much emphasis on learning because he would get made fun of and targeted within his gang.

Uriel's mother began to worry about him more and more and searched for a high school for Uriel to attend. She wanted a school that would teach him rather than punish him. Uriel wanted to go to his neighborhood school because that's where all his friends were going, but his mother succeeded in enrolling Uriel in Health Sciences High and Middle College, so that's where he began ninth grade.

A MEMBER OF THE SCHOOL STAFF STARTED ASKING URIEL WHAT HE WANTED TO DO WITH HIS LIFE—A QUESTION THAT NO ONE HAD EVER EARNESTLY ASKED URIEL BEFORE.

On the first day of school, there were tons of balloons and a red carpet leading to the entrance of the school. All the teachers were standing outside yelling and cheering and welcoming the students back from summer break. This surprised Uriel and lit a spark in him, but he didn't quite understand what that meant yet. His priority at that point in his life was to be the toughest, most known individual on the streets, and he continued to make sure his outside persona reflected that. He knew that with this persona came certain labels and assumptions about who he was, and, based on experience, he fully expected that it was only a matter of time before he was suspended, or maybe even expelled, from his new high school.

The school was located in the neighborhood of a rival gang, which, as the school year went on, proved difficult for Uriel. He had problems before and after school; rival gang members learned his class schedule, and he was often threatened by gang members yelling from just beyond the school grounds. As Uriel began to get in trouble, he fully expected to be treated as the "bad guy" he portrayed. However, that wasn't the case. Administrators and teachers began to ask him questions about what was going on, how he was feeling, and what they could do to help. This genuine concern and interest from people at the school shocked Uriel, and he began to realize that he was being seen as a human being, not just as a student involved in gangs.

"One thing that always impressed me was that my teachers didn't let my past dictate who I was at that point. I always felt the message," Uriel said, "that 'I care about you and your education. It doesn't matter who you are, where you come from, or what others think about you. You are important.'"

Uriel continued to build relationships with teachers and staff at Health Sciences High School and over time realized that school felt more like home to him than his actual home.

"It felt crazy to me that I was running to the school for support rather than my own family. I think that says a lot, especially from an individual from the streets. It's hard to leave that lifestyle," he said.

Teachers gave their time whenever he needed it, helped him when he didn't understand academic content, and never turned their backs when he made mistakes. Everyone in the building worked to learn his name and pronounce it correctly, which made him feel valued and that he belonged on campus. And he wasn't the only one—they treated all students this way.

Midway through junior year, Uriel began to realize that he didn't want to go down the gang path anymore. There were rival gang members who were threatening his life, and he knew that he didn't want to end up dead or in prison. He didn't want to make more choices or engage in more behavior that would hurt the people at school who genuinely cared about him, so he started to take steps away from gang life. It was at this same time that a member of the school staff started asking Uriel what he wanted to do with his life—a question that no one had ever earnestly asked Uriel before. Uriel voiced that he was interested in going into the U.S. Army, and the staff at school helped him research the requirements and get the ball rolling.

At that same time, Uriel's parents were detained and then deported, and Uriel had to take care of his little sister as well as get a job to support the two of them. Without the support of the school, Uriel would not have been able to accomplish his goals.

Upon graduation, Uriel was extremely proud of everything he had accomplished and excited about what was coming next in his life. But his joy was mixed with the reality that everyone in his family told him that day that they never thought he would graduate. The lack of confidence in him and his abilities stung and made an otherwise momentous day feel bittersweet.

Uriel joined the U.S. Army, but his family was not able to travel and see his promotion from boot camp. But a staff member from his high school stood there, cheering for him, congratulating him on the next phase of his life. Uriel served his country for four years.

"WITHOUT RESTORATIVE PRACTICES, I'D PROBABLY BE DEAD OR IN JAIL. IT REALLY DOES MATTER."

After four years in the Army, Uriel decided he wanted to work for U.S. Customs and Border Protection. To do that, he needed to get into law enforcement, so he began working as a security guard at Health Sciences High while he figured out the next steps to go to the police academy. It was just meant to be a temporary position to hold him over at a transitional time. Those plans quickly changed when he stepped back on campus. He fell in love again with the amazing work the school did with students and how supportive they were. He was home. Uriel is now a counselor at Health Sciences High and a walking testament to the power of restorative practices. He knows that there are a lot of students who need a lot of help, and he works daily to help them build their self-efficacy, reach their potential, and take ownership of themselves and their futures. In his own words: "I see a little bit of myself in all the students I work with now. And because of that, I know that they want help. They may not want to say it out loud, but I know it's true. The way I see it, I'm paying it back. People who didn't need to helped me when I needed it. Now it's my turn."

IDENTIFY A STUDENT YOU DON'T KNOW WELL AND FIND OUT ABOUT THEIR STORY.

As of this writing, we have known Uriel for 12 years. He did not think he was going to make it to this point in his life. He hurt a lot of feelings. He tried to destroy relationships and there were many bumps along the way as Uriel and the school found their way together. Now, he's a proud father and contributing member of society who supports his family and loves his life. As he says, "Without restorative practices, I'd probably be dead or in jail. It really does matter."

Thank you for reading about Uriel and his experiences. You will have your own and there will be students who return to thank you for not giving up on them, for helping them reach their goals, and for understanding when they made mistakes and even hurt your feelings.

We get a lot of questions about restorative practices. With Uriel's help, we have compiled some frequently asked questions and answers.

WHERE DO I FIND THE TIME TO DO THIS?

There is never a good time to do this. But consider how much time is already being consumed by reactive procedures that are oriented to finding a quick solution before moving on to the next problem. This is a process to grow into as a school. It begins with learning about restorative practices in general and in taking on incremental steps that lead you to your goals. As we advised in Module 1, developing a logic model can help with laying out a plan that works best for your context. As first steps, take an inventory and develop action steps toward developing a restorative culture. Perhaps the place to begin is in examining the ways that belonging, agency, and identities are fostered in your school.

HOW LONG DOES IT TAKE FOR A SCHOOL TO BECOME RESTORATIVE?

When we set out to become a restorative school nearly 15 years ago, we naively thought that a year of professional development would do the trick. We were wrong. In 2022, we continue this journey for a very valid reason that is often overlooked: schools are not static. Personnel change, students and families change, and even the demands of schooling change. And let's not forget that societal influences shape who all of us are. In the last several years we have witnessed political turmoil, the twin pandemics of coronavirus and racism, and major shifts in the economic lives of families. And let's not forget the demands of distance learning and how we rebound. The restorative practices lens we adopted in 2009 couldn't survive without a continual reinvestment and re-envisioning of a responsive system that meets students where they are and teaches them how to achieve their aspirations.

WHAT ADVICE DO YOU HAVE FOR PEOPLE WHO ARE NEW TO THIS?

Take an account of the processes you already have in place in your classroom and your school, noting areas of strength and growth opportunities. Now look again at those strengths and start there. Is there a successful initiative at your school about belonging? Look to enhance that further by taking steps to ensure that student voice is a part of it. Are you especially skilled at using affective statements with your students? Extend those by integrating impromptu conversations, 2 × 10s, or Banking Time into your classroom routine.

Above all, identify a student you don't know well and find out about their story. Uriel advises, "Get to know your students as human beings, not just as students. There are always external factors that affect students' behaviors, and you need to learn about those in order to help them."

WHAT DO YOU DO IF YOU DON'T THINK RESTORATIVE PRACTICES ARE MAKING A DIFFERENCE?

It's probably fair to say that as educators, we have all thrown our hands up in the air about a particular student. We've invested, guided, repaired, and restored—and still, that kid is making bad decisions. Having a team to turn to is incredibly valuable because the feeling that you're alone in the fight for a student is exhausting. When you reach those moments, talk with others who you trust with the work.

"Be patient," Uriel says. "I know we want to see changes right away, but it takes time. It took three years for me to really start making personal changes. Imagine if they had given up on me because I didn't change 'fast enough.'" He went on to say that his change was a gradual one that evolved over time. "I started to change myself when I realized the school wasn't a threatening place. In fact, it's weird, but it was exactly the opposite—school was welcoming and kind. I realized that I didn't need to be tough or scary in that environment. I could get rid of that defense mechanism and just be myself."

YOUR STORIES

"IMAGINE IF THEY HAD GIVEN UP ON ME BECAUSE I DIDN'T CHANGE 'FAST ENOUGH.'"
— URIEL CORTEZ

A moral reward we all draw upon as educators is the opportunity to have meaningful relationships with students. You have your own stories about the ways you have positively impacted students in ways large (like Uriel) and small (the student who comes back to hug you at the end of the day). But what if that impact could be systematized, instead of being left up to luck? Restorative practices are a systemic approach "to foster a relational-driven school community" (Kervick et al., 2020, p. 155). To paraphrase our own words: "Every student deserves a great education, not by chance but by design." How will you design that possibility in your classroom and school? We can't wait to learn from you.

REFERENCES

Adams, M., & Bell, L. A. (2016). *Teaching for diversity and social justice* (3rd ed.). Routledge.

Alamos, P., Williford, A. P., & LoCasale-Crouch, J. (2018). Understanding *banking time* implementation in a sample of preschool children who display early disruptive behaviors. *School Mental Health, 10*, 437–449. https://doi.org/10.1007/s12310-018-9260-9

Babad, E. (1998). Preferential effect: The crux of the teacher expectancy issue. In J. Brophy (Ed.), *Advances in research on teaching: Expectations in the classroom* (pp. 183–214). JAI Press.

Berry, A. (2020). Disrupting to driving: Exploring upper primary teachers' perspectives on student engagement. *Teachers and Teaching, 26*(2), 145–165. https://doi.org/10.1080/13540602.2020.1757421

California Teachers Association. (2019, December 12). Restorative practices after a disaster. *California Educator*. https://www.cta.org/educator/posts/trauma-restorative-practices.

Center for Advanced Study of Teaching and Learning. (n.d.). *Learning to objectively observe kids (LOOK)*. www.lookconsultation.org

Chew, S. L., & Cerbin, W. J. (2020). The cognitive challenges of effective teaching. *Journal of Economic Education*. https://doi.org/10.1080/00220485.2020.1845266

Costello, B., Wachtel, J., & Wachtel, T. (2009). *Restorative practices handbook for teachers, disciplinarians and administrators*. International Institute for Restorative Practices.

Darby, M. W. (2021). Ending the school-to-prison pipeline in South Carolina through legislative reform. *Journal of Law & Education, 50*(2), 390–423.

Driscoll, K. C., &. Pianta, R. C. (2010). Banking time in head start: Early efficacy of an intervention designed to promote supportive teacher–child relationships. *Early Education and Development, 21*(1), 38–64. https://doi.org/10.1080/10409280802657449

Finnis, M. (2021). *Restorative practice*. Independent Thinking.

Fisher, D., & Frey, N. (2021). Why do students disengage? *Educational Leadership*. https://www.ascd.org/el/articles/show-and-tell-a-video-column-why-do-students-disengage

Fisher, D., Frey, N., Quaglia, R. J., Smith, D., & Lande, L. L. (2017). *Engagement by design: Creating learning environments where students thrive*. Corwin.

Fisher, D., Frey, N., Smith, D., & Hattie, J. (2021). *Rebound: A playbook for rebuilding agency, accelerating learning recovery, and rethinking schools*. Corwin.

Fletcher, A. (2005). *Meaningful school involvement: Guide to students as partners in school change* (2nd ed.). The Freechild Project. https://soundout.org/wp-content/uploads/2015/06/MSIGuide.pdf.

Fronius, T., Darling-Hammond, S., Persson, H., Guckenburg, S., Hurley, N., & Petrosino, A. (2019). *Restorative justice in U.S. schools: An updated research review*. WestEd Justice & Prevention Research Center. https://www.wested.org/wp-content/uploads/2019/04/resource-restorative-justice-in-u-s-schools-an-updated-research-review.pdf

Ginsberg, M., & Wlodkowski, R. (2004). *Creating highly motivating classrooms*. Jossey Bass.

González, T., Sattler, H., & Buth, A. J. (2019). New directions in whole-school restorative justice implementation. *Conflict Resolution Quarterly, 36*(3), 207–220.

Goodenow, C. (1993). Classroom belonging among early adolescent students: Relationships to motivation and achievement. *Journal of Early Adolescence, 13*(1), 21–43. https://doi.org/10.1177/0272431693013001002

Gordon, T. (2003). *Teacher effectiveness training: The program proven to help teachers bring out the best in students of all ages*. Three Rivers Press.

Gregory, A., Clawson, K., Davis, A., & Gerewitz, J. (2016). The promise of restorative practices to transform teacher–student relationships and achieve equity in school discipline. *Journal of Educational and Psychological Consultation, 26*(4), 325–353. https://doi.org/10.1080/10474412.2014.929950

Gregory, A., Skiba, R. J., & Noguera, P. A. (2010). The achievement gap and the discipline gap: Two sides of the same coin? *Educational Researcher, 39*(1), 59–68. https://doi.org/10.3102/0013189X09357621.

Griffiths, C. T., & Cunningham, A. H. (2007). *Canadian criminal justice: A primer* (6th ed.). Thomson Nelson.

Hamre, B. K., Pianta, R. C., Downer, J. T., DeCoster, J., Mashburn, A. J., Jones, S. M., Brown, J. L., Cappella, E., Atkins, M., Rivers, S. E., Brackett, M. A., & Hamagami, A. (2013). Teaching through Interactions. *Elementary School Journal, 113*(4), 461–487.

Hargraves, V. (2018). High expectations self-assessment checklist. How to develop high expectation teaching. *The Education Hub*. https://theeducationhub.org.nz/how-to-develop-high-expectations-teaching.

Illinois Balanced and Restorative Justice (n.d.). *Restorative practices in schools implementation checklist*. http://www.restorativeschoolstoolkit.org/sites/default/files/RP%20in%20Schools%20Implementation%20Checklist.pdf

Iowa State University, Center for Excellence in Learning and Teaching. (2021). *Reflect on your sense of belonging practices*. https://www.celt.iastate.edu/wp-content/uploads/2021/07/sense-of-belonging-practices.pdf

Julian, D. (1997). The utilization of the logic model as a system level planning and evaluation device. *Evaluation and Program Planning, 20*(3), 251–257.

Kervick, C. T., Garnett, B., Moore, M., Ballysingh, T. A., & Smith, L. C. (2020). Introducing restorative practices in a diverse elementary school to build community and reduce exclusionary discipline: Year one processes, facilitators, and next steps. *School Community Journal, 30*(2), 155–183.

Kowalski, M., & Froiland, J. (2020). Parent perceptions of elementary classroom management systems and their children's motivational and emotional responses. *Social Psychology of Education, 23*(5). 10.1007/s11218-020-09543-5.

Langley, J. (2016). *Restorative practices in the early years: Visual scripts*. Small World.

Mehrabian, A. (1971). *Silent messages*. Wadsworth.

Meiners, C. J. (2005). *Talk and work it out*. Free Spirit Publishing.

Oakland Unified School District. (n.d.). *Restorative justice implementation guide: A whole school approach*. https://www.ousd.org/cms/lib/CA01001176/Centricity/Domain/134/BTC-OUSD1-IG-08b-web.pdf

OECD (n.d). *OECD future of education and skills 2030: Student agency*. https://www.oecd.org/education/2030-project/teaching-and-learning/learning/student-agency

Pipas, C. F., & Pepper, E. (2021). Building community well-being through emotional intelligence and cognitive reframing: With communities facing so much unrest, here are two skills you can apply to help promote healing. *Family Practice Management, 28*(1), 23.

Positive Behaviour for Learning. (2014a). *Restorative practice kete book two: Restorative essentials*. New Zealand Ministry of Education.

Positive Behaviour for Learning. (2014b). *Restorative practice kete book three: Restorative circles*. New Zealand Ministry of Education.

Purkey, W. W., & Novak, J. M. (1996). *Inviting school success: A self-concept approach to teaching, learning, and democratic practice* (3rd ed.). Wadsworth Publishing.

Rubie-Davies, C. (2014). *Becoming a high expectation teacher: Raising the bar*. Routledge.

Shawley, J. (n.d.). *Building relationships with students: The 2 × 10 theory*. blog.gophersport.com/connecting-with-students-the-2x10-theory

Skrzypek, C., Bascug, E. W., Ball, A., Kim, W., & Elze, D. (2020). In their own words: Student perceptions of restorative practices. *Children & Schools, 42*(4), 245–253.

Smith, D., Fisher, D., & Frey, N. (2015). *Better than carrots or sticks: Restorative practices for positive classroom management*. ASCD.

Smith, D., Fisher, D., & Frey, N. (2021). *Removing labels, grades K–12: 40 techniques to disrupt negative expectations about students and schools*. Corwin.

Thorsborne, M., & Blood, P. (2013). *Implementing restorative practice in schools: A practical guide to transforming school communities*. Kingsley.

Thorsborne, M., & Vinegrad, D. (2004). *Restorative practice in schools: Rethinking behaviour management*. Inyahead Press.

Tomkins, S. S. (1962). *Affect imagery consciousness: The positive affects*. Springer.

United Nations Office on Drugs and Crime. (2006). *Handbook on restorative justice programs*. Author. www.unodc.org/pdf/criminal_justice/Handbook_on_Restorative_Justice_Programmes.pdf

Vaughn, M., Premo, J., Sotirovska, V. V., & Erickson, D. (2020). Evaluating agency in literacy using the Student Agency Profile. *Reading Teacher, 73*(4), 427–441.

Wachtel, T., O'Connell, T., & Wachtel, B. (2010). *Restorative justice conferencing*. International Institute for Restorative.

Wangberg, J. K. (1996). Teaching with a passion. *American Entomologist, 42,* 199–200.

Washington State Governor's Office of the Education Ombuds (n.d.). *Reengagement planning after long-term suspension or expulsion*. www.oeo.wa.gov/en/education-issues/discipline-suspensions-and-expulsions/reengagement-planning-after-long-term

Welsh, R. O., & Little, S. (2018). The school discipline dilemma: A comprehensive review of disparities and alternative approaches. *Review of Educational Research, 88*(5), 752–794. https://doi.org/10.3102/0034654318791582

What Ed Said. (2014). *10 tips for creating a class agreement*. whatedsaid.wordpress.com/2014/01/26/10-tips-for-creating-a-class-agreement

Whiting, E. F., Everson, K. C., & Feinauer, E. (2018). The simple school belonging scale: Working toward a unidimensional measure of student belonging. *Measurement & Evaluation in Counseling & Development, 51*(3), 163–178. https://doi.org/10.1080/07481756.2017.1358057

Willcox, G. (1982). The feeling wheel: A tool for expanding awareness of emotions and increasing spontaneity and intimacy. *Transactional Analysis Journal, 12*(4), 274–276. https://doi.org/10.1177/036215378201200411

Zeiser, K., Scholz, C., & Cirks, V. (2018). *Maximizing student agency: Implementing and measuring student-centered learning practices*. American Institutes of Research. https://files.eric.ed.gov/fulltext/ED592084.pdf

INDEX

CORWIN
A SAGE Publishing Company

Helping educators make the greatest impact

CORWIN HAS ONE MISSION: to enhance education through intentional professional learning.

We build long-term relationships with our authors, educators, clients, and associations who partner with us to develop and continuously improve the best evidence-based practices that establish and support lifelong learning.

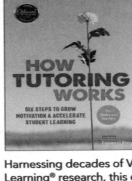